The Great NEW YORK DOG BOOK

Enjoy!

Deb & Serena

The Great
NEW YORK
DOG BOOK

The Indispensable Canine Resource Guide
for New York City Dogs and Their Owners

DEBORAH LOVEN

📖 HarperPerennial
A Division of HarperCollins*Publishers*

For Phebe,
who lives on in beautiful Serena.

HarperCollins books may be purchased for educational, business, or sales promotional use. For information, please write: Special Markets Department, HarperCollins Publishers, Inc., 10 East 53rd Street, New York, NY 10022.

FIRST EDITION

Designed by Charles Kreloff

Library of Congress Cataloging-in-Publication Data

Loven, Deborah, 1963–
    The great New York dog book : the indispensable canine resource guide for New York City dogs and their owners / Deborah Loven. — 1st ed.
        p.   cm.
    Includes index.
    ISBN 0-06-095092-7
    1. Dogs—New York (N.Y.)   I. Title
SF427.L68   1995
636.7'009747'1—dc20   95-15536

95 96 97 98 99 ❖/RRD 10 9 8 7 6 5 4 3 2 1

Contents

Cover dog, Daisy, is a classic New York story. Abandoned at a Manhattan veterinary hospital, she found a loving home on the very day she was to be surrendered to a shelter. Her new owner, Laura, had never had a dog before, but after one look into Daisy's eyes, she couldn't resist. What makes their meeting even more symbolic is that Laura adopted Daisy on October 4, St. Francis of Assisi Day. Laura saved Daisy, and Daisy opened Laura's life to the joy of owning a dog in New York City.

Acknowledgments

I would like to thank some of the many people whose hard work, enthusiasm, and support made this book possible: Phyllis Levy, Pam Bernstein, Paul Coughlin, Jim Dratfield, and Robin Kovary; my friends at the Fidelco Guide Dog Foundation, Guiding Eyes for the Blind, Connecticut Valley Dog Training, and Ford Models; intrepid helpers Lauren Segan, Ed Corley, Josh Gray, Maria Olivas, and Joan Wargo; Laura Reckford and Daisy; Irene Rivera and Spunky; and wonderful Robert Jones and Scout! Thanks most of all to my parents, who cheerfully accommodated the many animals—from ducks to thoroughbreds—that I brought them.

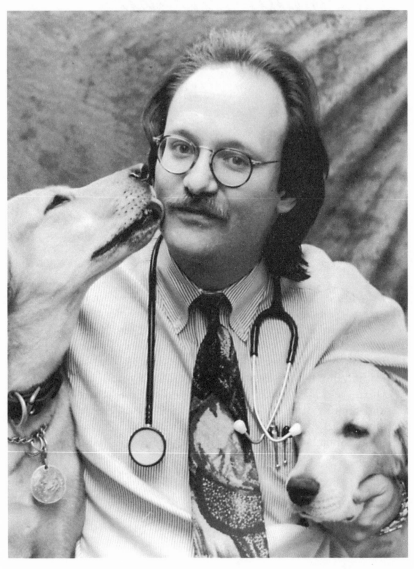

V.C. gives Dr. Solomon a kiss while his other dog, golden retriever Biscuit, sneaks her nose into the picture.   Credit: Petography

Introduction

By Gene A. Solomon, D.V.M.

My own dog was my first patient. The story of how V.C., my yellow Lab mix, found her way to me is a classic New York example of the relationship between dogs and people.

Eight years ago, a client of mine was riding in a New York cab with her dog, and she got in a conversation with the driver. He confided that he was very upset because his dog had a litter of six-week-old puppies, and three days before, one of the pups had gotten out of the house and been hit by a car. He knew the pup was hurt, but he didn't know exactly what to do. "Why, you've got to take her to Dr. Solomon!" advised my client.

It was the week before my partner, Paul Schwartz, and I opened our own practice, the Center for Veterinary Care. I happened to be in the office that night, taking inventory of our new equipment, when the cabbie knocked at the door. Following the advice the woman had given him, he had taken time from his shift and driven home to the Bronx to pick up the pup and bring her to me. Double-parked and very stressed, he seemed at a loss. The puppy was seriously injured, the cabbie had very little money, and he didn't even know what he was going to do with the *healthy* pups in the litter.

When I saw the puppy, she looked closer to Bambi than anything else I'd ever seen. Her big brown eyes with golden lashes and her thumping tail almost drew your attention away from her obviously broken and gangrenous leg.

"Don't worry," I told the cabbie, "I'll take her."

"You'll put her to sleep?" he asked.

"No, no, I'll fix her leg, if I can, and find her a home."

He smiled with relief and handed her over.

We worked for a few weeks trying to save the leg. No matter how many times we cleaned or wrapped it, the puppy never flinched. As I've seen so many times with animals, it was as though she *knew* we were trying to help her. When the gangrene became a threat, we decided to amputate; I took the leg off myself. Always a trooper, she came out of the anesthesia and acted as though she had been born with three legs.

By this time, my promise to the cabbie was fulfilled. Since she was our first patient, we didn't yet have personnel to care for her when we weren't at the office, so I kept her with me. By the time the Center for Veterinary Care actually opened, the puppy was already a fixture. We started calling her V.C., short for the center's name, and it stuck. *She* greeted the new staff members and clients when they arrived. I couldn't bear to find her another home. A new business needs a mascot. She was my dog.

I am not a native New Yorker, but this is the only place I would ever want to practice veterinary medicine. Every day I have the privilege of observing and working with New York dogs and their owners. I get the chance to see the deep bond that they share. The caring and empathetic nature of this relationship makes my job easier. New Yorkers are unusually attuned to their dogs, and when they know what to do, or where to go, they are quick to act on their pets' behalf.

This is what makes *The Great New York Dog Book* so important. Here you will find the advice and resources to be an excellent dog owner. I'm pretty lucky; I get to treat New York dogs. And, thanks to a client's recommendation, I take one home too. I hope that this book helps you to enjoy your pet as much as I enjoy V.C.

Preface

You want a dog. You want a companion, a pet, a friend, a kindred spirit, a pal, a protector, a workout buddy, an unconflicted heart, a reason to get out of the house, a silent partner, a worshiper, a true-blue, when-the-chips-are-down amigo! You want a dog. But you live in New York City, where conventional wisdom (and perhaps your own common sense) dictates that: NYC + DOG = BAD IDEA.

The anti-dog-in-town rap goes something like this: "I love dogs, but I think it's cruel to keep one in an apartment." Or, "Dogs need to be in the country where they can run free." Or, "Life in the city is just too frantic for a dog." These are legitimate views, but they tell only part of the story.

We often think it's cruel and unusual punishment to box *ourselves* in the tiny spaces that New York apartments usually offer, so why would we subject an animal to the same conditions, particularly a dog bigger than a bread box? We have visions of Lassie, proud and free, bounding across a golden meadow of heather. Surely a dog needs liberty to run and hunt if it chooses? How can the asphalt of New York compare to fields and woods? It's garbage collection night, and although you have wangled an apartment in the most enviable neighborhood, under your window it sounds as though a herd of elephants is running amok in a tin factory. The trumpeting of brakes and the banging of trash cans is unbearable, then a car alarm goes off! You are going half-mad yourself and wouldn't dream of subjecting a pet to such mayhem.

Yes, our urban landscape is at best an asphalt jungle, not the forest or the moors. For a total stress package, no other city beats New York. Why on earth subject a pet to this madness? Dogs don't exactly get to enjoy the trade-offs that keep us here: the diversity, the business world, the restaurants, or the arts. What's in it for them, and why on earth would we, as thoughtful, loving (potential) dog owners, ever consider having them here?

There is one truth about New York: Anything is possible, and that includes the ability to keep a happy, healthy dog. You simply need common sense and a little help. The guidance and support I'll give you in this book, and the network of dog friends and professionals you will meet through it, will supply the help. I trust you for the common sense.

First of all, let's look at where dogs come from. Despite the proportions of a Pekingese or a Pomeranian, all domesticated dogs evolved from wild wolves. Wolves are intensely social animals. They live in packs, generally comprising a family group, with two leaders, or alphas, one male and one female. These represent Mom and Dad—the authority figures. Also in the group are a new litter of pups each year (kids to be raised), the odd adolescent ("Just not ready for college yet, Dad, can I still live in my room?"), and sometimes another mature male or female ("Now, your great-aunt Tillie is coming to live with us, and I want you to treat her with the same respect you give your father and me.") This hierarchy maintains order, and allows the group to function as a unit, thereby affording it the maximum chance for survival in the wild. The wolf world is complex and social: They communicate, interact, defend their territory, fall in love, fight, raise young, cooperate, hunt, and grieve.

About 12,000 years ago, wolf pups joined the human community. *Exactly* how this happened will always be a mystery, but following their natural instincts, the pups protected their adopted human pack, hunted with them, and generally made themselves useful. Eventually man began to raise and selectively mate the tamed wolf pups' offspring for specific character traits, things like loyalty, protection, herding ability, hunting, and retrieving. This process brought us different breeds of dog with distinct talents for different kinds of work or sport. By the time the pyramids were being built, the sleek pharaoh hound accompanied the kings and princes of Egypt. When the Roman legions marched, sturdy mastiffs were suited in armor to fight alongside their masters. A spaniel and a retriever arrived from England on the *Mayflower*. Today we have over four hundred recognized breeds of domesticated dog, all descended from—and still able to crossbreed with—wolves.

So dogs have been designed to live with, and serve, us. We are their adopted pack; they have accepted our society as their own. Our concerns are their concerns. They love us, want to be with us, and value our company.

But that still doesn't explain why you should keep one in New York.

Of course New York apartments are small, but the issue of confinement really comes down to a question of exercise. If a city dog has sufficient opportunity to exercise and evacuate, the actual size of his living space is immaterial. As long as he goes out several times a day, the city dog is free to do what dogs naturally do when they are relaxed: lie around dozing. Even suburban dogs spend the day lying around while the family is at work or school. Most city dogs have the option of loafing about on comfortable furniture, unlike their country cousins who are often relegated to the Siberia of an undecorated doghouse in the backyard.

The vision of a dog running happily through the woods or fields is beautiful, but it's unrealistic. Dogs who are allowed to roam loose in the country are routinely killed or maimed by cars, injured in fights with other animals, shot for trespassing, sprayed by skunks and porcupines, or lost. If the city dog owner accommodates the needs of her dog with a daily long walk or run, the dog won't be missing anything.

Of course the traffic, noise, and confusion of New York is disorienting and stressful, but everyone grows accustomed to it. A country dog who moves to the city will need a period of adjustment during which she can gently be introduced to street life, but most dogs acclimate beautifully to the hustle and bustle. Dogs are extremely gregarious, and puppies raised here accept the pace as the norm. Remember, hunting and military dogs constantly work under gunfire with no ill effects. As any out of towner who moves to the Big Apple knows, it's all a matter of conditioning.

The concerns which may have prevented you from keeping a

dog in New York City are sincere, but can be remedied, and there are compelling reasons *to* have a dog in town.

Dogs love city life because they love humans. No city dog is left to pine for its family at the end of a chain beside a doghouse or is locked out in a kennel. Happily for the dog, due to the confines of apartment living, the metropolitan dog is always fully integrated into its family's daily life. A dog doesn't care if he lives in a tiny studio in the East Village, or a sprawling Park Avenue penthouse, as long as it is full of the people he loves.

New Yorkers are a diverse group. Many are self-employed or work odd hours, making them free in the daytime to explore with their dogs. If you work conventional hours, and want your dog to get out in the middle of the day, there are many relatively inexpensive dog-walking services that will exercise your dog. Even "doggie day care" is available in New York. You drop your dog off at the day care center on your way to work, and he spends the day playing with other dogs, having a snack at lunchtime, sleeping, and watching television (reportedly *101 Dalmatians* on video and "Lassie" television reruns are preferred). Show me a New York lifestyle, and I'll show you a way to accommodate a dog.

New York dogs are suave and confident. They're constantly out and about, meeting and greeting new dogs, neighbors, passersby, and children. The city dog rides with its owner in taxis; eats al fresco at outdoor cafes and bars, where he is treated and toasted; goes to street fairs and outdoor concerts; shops at Bergdorf's and Banana Republic. Some dogs summer in the Hamptons and are flown to Aspen for the holidays; some attend downtown poetry readings, or wait patiently backstage at the Metropolitan Opera as their owner sings an aria. New York dogs have play groups and play dates (when my dog, Serena, and I moved to town, she had three play dates in the first week! Needless to say, my social calendar could not compete); they go to private groomers, doggie birthday (and any other holiday) parties, and special events. In short, the life of the New York dog is every bit as interesting as that of its owner.

Statistically, city dogs are healthier and live longer than their rural cousins. I won't say that New Yorkers are obsessive, but we tend to be *keenly absorbed* with things that interest us. This spells good fortune for a pet. The New Yorker with the dedication to keep a dog in the city usually makes for a very committed owner. We search for the best foods for our dogs, fulfill their exercise and social needs, and monitor any changes in their habits and moods that might signal illness. We are prompt to act, and have the best medical care in the world readily available for our pets. Since city dogs are constantly supervised, they lead much safer lives. The quality of life of the New York City dog can be the best. They live the high life.

Now, how to do it?

Read this book. Allow me to take you by the hand and lead you through the process of acquiring and keeping a dog in New York City. I'll give you the resources, direction, and contacts you'll need to make the job a delight. Continue to use *The Great New York Dog Book* as a guide and faithful reference for all the questions and concerns you have about your dog-about-town. Advice and support will be yours, and along the way I'll introduce you to some of your new peers: other famous and interesting New York dog lovers. By the time you and your pet finish reading *The Great New York Dog Book*, New York City life with a dog will be such a pleasure, you'll be ready for canine companion number two! Enjoy.

The Great New York Mayor, Rudolph Giuliani, and the family dog, Goalie. Bred as a potential guide dog by Guiding Eyes for the Blind, in Yorktown Heights, Goalie was adopted by the Giuliani family. Credit: NY Post

Chapter 1

So, You Want to Get a Dog

There are as many reasons to share your life in New York with a dog as there are opening nights on Broadway. Do you see happy pairs of dogs and owners parading around your neighborhood and feel a little left out? Does the memory of your own wonderful childhood pet haunt you? Are your kids lobbying hard for a dog? Do you catch yourself gushing over new puppies you meet, and only smiling vaguely at a friend's new baby? Just last night, after the Chinese food deliveryman brought your usual order of General Tso's Chicken, did you suddenly notice that *nobody barked* when he buzzed your intercom?

For companionship, affection, protection, involvement, and fun, opening your life to a dog can be a joy. So, after careful deliberation, you decided to get a(nother) dog. Now what do you do?

Well, what kind of dog do you want? Do you have misty fantasies of running around the reservoir with a flashy Irish setter, your collective hairs blowing in the wind? Do you picture yourself, scotch in hand, seated by a fireplace in an English manor house, your spaniel flopped adoringly at your feet? Does the image of yourself window-shopping on Madison Avenue with a bright-eyed, beribboned Yorkie cradled in your arm appeal to you? Whatever you envision, the key is to discover what kind of dog would suit *you* and your *lifestyle*.

What Exactly Are You Looking For?

Let's start with what sort of dog would best suit you. Take a realistic look at your lifestyle. Do you have the time for a new puppy? Sure, they're adorable, but like any baby, they demand *even more* commitment and attention than a mature dog would. An older dog will probably be housebroken and have some basic training, but plenty of energy will still have to be spent getting her adjusted to life with you.

Any dog will make a loving pal, but if you're considering a purebred, you have the opportunity to choose the canine traits and talents you want. Remember that different breeds have been bred for generations for specific talents. For example, herding breeds, like collies and shepherds, have been bred for watching and guarding sheep, so they are particularly vigilant and protective. Sporting breeds, like goldens and Labs, were bred for fetching game, so they love, love, *love* to retrieve. The toy breeds—pugs and Pekingese, for example—were sometimes guard dogs, and make compact, clever companions. Keep these "breed stereotypes" in mind when making your decision.

If you decide on a purebred dog, it is important to remember that almost every breed has some medical "Achilles heel," a common genetic problem that is passed on from generation to generation. Many large breeds, like Labs and shepherds, are prone to arthritis, while some of the smaller breeds, like bulldogs and dachshunds, often suffer from spinal problems. Books about the different breeds will inform you on these medical issues, and a vet should be able to help you with advice as well. The more you know, the more informed the questions you can ask.

Mixed breed dogs have a wonderful "hybrid vigor" that usually makes them especially healthy and intelligent pets.

As a New Yorker, you've probably undertaken an exhaustive quest for the perfect bagel (I vote for H & H on Broadway—if you can stand the long lines!). Why shouldn't you be as obsessive about finding the dog of your dreams? A good place to start is **The American Kennel Club (AKC) Customer Service Department,** 919-233-9767. They'll supply you with an infor-

What Is a "Registered" Dog, Anyway?

Dogs are often advertised as being "registered." This simply means that both parents were enrolled in one of the breed registries and that the dog's lineage can be verified and traced. Registering a dog is not necessarily a stamp of quality or a guarantee that the dog will be free of problems. The registries only oversee pedigrees; they do not supervise how healthily or ethically the dogs are bred.

The predominant all-breed registry in this country is **The American Kennel Club,** 51 Madison Avenue, 20th floor, New York, NY 10010, 212-696-8245 or 919-233-9767, which sanctions dog shows and competitions for its members. **The United Kennel Club,** 100 East Kilgore Road, Kalamazoo, MI 49001, 616-343-9020, is the second-largest all-breed registry, as well as the largest working dog registry, meaning that more people who compete in events that test their dogs' working abilities register with the UKC and attend their sanctioned events.

If you have a mixed breed, don't despair! Your dog may be registered with **AMBOR, The American Mixed Breed Obedience Registration,** 205 1st Street S.W., New Prague, MN 56071, 612-758-4598, or **The Mixed Breed Dog Club of America,** 1937 Seven Pines Drive, St. Louis, MO 63146.

mation packet full of flyers, from "Do You Really Want to Own a Dog?" to "Choosing the Right Breeder." Included will be a geographical listing of dog clubs where you can obtain even more information.

Why not hire a canine "headhunter" to help you in your quest? Samantha Cannon at **Your Best Friend Personalized Canine Selection,** P.O. Box 188966, Sacramento, CA 95818, 916-682-3880, is a dog trainer with a background in psychology and social work. She counsels prospective owners, analyzing their lifestyles and wishes, and matches them up with the dog breed best suited to them. For a $20 fee she sends you a detailed personal profile questionnaire. From your responses, she suggests three breeds from the 144 different varieties recognized by The American Kennel Club and the United Kennel Club. Included are profile sheets on each of the three breeds, as well as information guiding you through the process of getting and keeping a dog.

Now, Where to Go

Once you have an idea about the *kind* of dog you want, where are you going to find her? A shelter? A rescue group? A guide or service dog school? A professional breeder? You know that the young couple in 16F got their golden retriever from a breeder upstate, but the adorable poodle in 4B came from a shelter, and you caught a glimpse of an abandoned dog running across the avenue last night. Might you have tried to catch it, and brought it home? There seem to be dogs *everywhere* in New York, but where should you look to find one?

Adopting from a Shelter

New Yorkers are famous for their big hearts, and the shelters in the metropolitan area are full of homeless dogs to fill them. These organizations deal daily with New York's overwhelming pet overpopulation problem and abandoned or abused animals. They *always* have wonderful, healthy, loving dogs available for adoption. Each provides back-up services to the adoptees, such as free or low-cost spay/neuter clinics, and continuing education, to help ensure a successful pairing of pet and owner.

When you're adopting a previously owned pet, understand that she may come with some special "baggage," and I don't mean Louis Vuitton! More often than not, owners surrender their pets to shelters when the dog exhibits behavior that the owner can't cope with. As a responsible new owner, you must take the time and energy to address your pet's problems and work to correct them. It could be something as simple as a dog who barked and chewed out of boredom after being left alone for hours and hours. Rather than providing exercise and stimulation for the dog in his absence—a midday jaunt with a dog walker and lots of new toys, for instance—the previous owner abandoned the pet. You should be prepared to seek guidance and help from the shelter's training staff.

Although a dog "with a history" is more of a challenge, she can be a diamond in the rough. Many people feel that rescued dogs somehow understand the fate they escaped, and in their gratitude, lavish special love and devotion on their new owners!

The ASPCA

The American Society for the Prevention of Cruelty to Animals, 326 East 110th Street, between 1st and 2nd avenues, New York, NY 10029, 212-722-3620; 424 East 92nd Street, New York, NY 10128, 212-876-7700; and 2336 Linden Boulevard, Brooklyn, NY 11208, 718-272-7200, cares for over 100,000 animals through their New York City shelters and veterinary hospitals. The legal department in the Manhattan office advises pet owners with legal problems, while the Washington office works on the federal level on behalf of animals. The Manhattan Adoption Center, on East 110th Street, is open from 11:00 A.M. to 7:00 P.M.

To adopt a dog, a $55 donation is required—after a strict screening process! The animal placement personnel want that new home to be the dog's *permanent* residence. At adoption time, expect to be asked for two forms of identification, one with your current address, and a personal reference who can be reached by telephone. Puppies, and purebreds without papers, are often available. If you are interested in adopting a puppy, the ASPCA personnel will expect someone in your household to be home during the day to supervise his housebreaking and early training.

Low-cost or free spaying and neutering, and other medical care, is done at the ASPCA's **Bergh Memorial Animal Hospital,** 424 East 92nd Street, New York, NY, 10029, 212-876-7700. **The Companion Animal Services Behavior Helpline,** 212-876-7700, ext. HELP (4357), open weekdays from 1:00 to 5:00 P.M., offers free advice and referrals to pet owners with problems. At the same number, you can get information on the plethora of useful and interesting training classes and programs. These are open to everyone but are available at a discount to dogs adopted from the ASPCA.

Bide-A-Wee

The Bide-A-Wee Home Association, 410 East 38th Street, New York, NY 10016, east of First Avenue, 212-532-4455, is open for adoptions Monday through Saturday, from 10:00 A.M. to 6:00 P.M., and Sundays from 10:00 A.M. to 5:00 P.M. Bide-A-

Wee's chief function is to find new homes for dogs and cats whose original owners can't keep them. They do not accept abandoned or stray animals, and an owner wanting to get rid of his dog or cat must make an appointment. Only after a screening process, and if space permits, is the pet accepted. Bide-A-Wee will care for the pet until a suitable new home can be found.

Bide-A-Wee also has two shelter/clinics on Long Island, in **Wantagh,** 516-785-4079, and **Westhampton,** 516-325-0200.

Because animals are admitted into Bide-A-Wee from their original owners, there is usually more information available about their medical and temperamental histories. This knowledge is invaluable to the prospective new owner, who can use it to effectively address any behavioral problems the pet may have had.

To adopt a pet from a Bide-A-Wee shelter, be prepared with two forms of identification, proof of employment, permanent address, and landlord's phone number. There is an interview. The adoption fee is $55 for dogs under six months (who will be spayed/neutered for free at the clinic) and $30 for older dogs who are already spayed/neutered. Low-cost medical care is available at the clinics, as are back-up services and training classes. Bide-A-Wee frequently has purebred dogs available for adoption, and sometimes puppies. Since its founding in 1903, Bide-A-Wee has placed over a million dogs in happy, permanent new homes. Perhaps your dream dog is waiting for you there right now!

The Humane Society

The Humane Society of New York's Adoption Center/ Clinic, 306 East 59th Street, New York, NY 10022, between 1st and 2nd avenues, in Manhattan, 212-752-4840, was founded in 1904 to protect New York City's horses from abuse. Since then it has set a standard for quality animal care. Today its two main areas of operation are as a hospital and a shelter for homeless pets.

Animals at The Humane Society get *lots* of individual attention from staff and volunteers. The day we visited, we were joined in conference by five or six happy cats—Pee Wee,

Tyrone, Luciana, Charlotte, and Eartha Kitten, a few of the many "seniors" that enjoy the run of the office. The shelter, which operates on a no-kill basis, is a loving, safe refuge for pets. Each animal's needs are evaluated and accommodated. There are separate "nursery" and "retirement" areas for juniors and seniors. Abused or handicapped dogs or cats who are not able to be adopted are cared for either at the Society, or in the homes of staff and volunteers.

All new arrivals are given a medical exam and shots. Adults are spayed/neutered prior to adoption, while the adopters of pets under six months of age must show proof of subsequent spaying/neutering.

Tales from The Humane Society

Abandoned in the Brownsville section of Brooklyn, the pregnant Border collie had been living off scraps of food from trash cans. When her time came, she had her litter of black and white puppies in a large drainpipe and began the grueling process of scavenging for her family.

At first things went all right. The pups stayed in the denlike pipe while she was away, and since she had some physical reserves from her years as a pet dog, she was able to give most of the food she found to her pups. The problems started when the whelps became mobile. Naturally, they followed their mother, and as many times as she would patiently carry them back to the den in her mouth, they would toddle after her.

A dog lover in the neighborhood had glimpsed the bitch foraging a few times. When the concerned New Yorker came across the bodies of two puppies in the road, she guessed what the situation was and looked for the den. The puppies were being killed by cars as they trotted after their mother. Unable to locate the litter, the Samaritan called The Humane Society.

Help arrived, and a concerted effort was launched to find the family. As the rescue party looked for the little group, they came across a most chilling sight: a dead puppy riddled with bullet wounds. In an appalling act of brutality, someone had used the little pup for target practice.

The rescuers soon found the mother and her three surviving puppies and took them to The Humane Society. Despite their wild beginnings, the pups were quite healthy and were quickly adopted. The mother dog was named "Mae," and after she recovered from her ordeal, she found a loving home with one of The Humane Society volunteers who had helped rescue her.

Once a bright-eyed, white toy poodle, "Little Girl" was found abandoned and wandering on Manhattan's Lower East Side. Her calm, loving manner told of happy associations with people, but by the time she arrived at The Humane Society, the months she had spent on the streets had taken their toll. Emaciated and nearly blind from cataracts, it took several weeks and the special care of The Humane Society's veterinarians and staff to bring her back to health.

About the time Little Girl was ready to find a home, the Society received a phone call from New York radio and television personality Joan Hamburg offering to host a Humane Society pet on her popular WOR-AM morning radio talk show. Active in the animal welfare community, Hamburg frequently does what she can to bring the plight of homeless animals to the public eye. On this occasion, she wanted a sweet, adoptable pet to share the studio with her as she went on the air and spoke about homeless animals. Susan Richmond at The Humane Society immediately thought of Little Girl, and on the appointed day she took her, freshly groomed and fully recovered from a cataract operation, to the studio.

Little Girl sat on Joan's lap and took everything in like a pro, sniffing and licking the microphone almost on cue. The power of radio worked, and they soon got a call from a listener in New Jersey who was interested in adopting the poodle. The caller was the retired mother superior of a convent who was now living on the grounds of a Catholic school. She wanted an older dog for companionship and could offer room to run and plenty of love. It seemed a perfect match, and sure enough, the next day a proverbial vanload of nuns arrived at The Humane Society's East 59th Street shelter to meet Little Girl. The mother superior and the other sisters fell in love with the adorable poodle on sight and promptly adopted her. Little Girl was fortunate enough to get a second chance and heartily returned the love and affection she received in her new home.

Open for adoptions weekdays from 11:00 A.M. until 4:00 P.M., and 10:00 A.M. until 2:00 P.M. weekends, The Humane Society requires a pre-adoption interview, so come prepared with proof of present address (a postmarked utility bill will do). The adoption fee is $65, which includes three weeks of free medical care through the Society's clinic. Should the new home not work out for any reason, it is a condition of the adoption contract that the pet be returned directly to The Humane Society.

They frequently have purebred dogs, and sometimes puppies, for adoption. At the time of my visit, they had recently placed dalmatians, Old English sheepdogs, pugs, varieties of poodles, a Shiba Inu, and bassets, as well as some wonderful "Heinz 57s." If you are interested in a specific breed which is not available at the time of your visit, you may put your name on a waiting list to be notified when that type of animal comes in.

The Humane Society also offers excellent low-cost veterinary care to all animals. Owners in extreme circumstances may apply for help from the Society's Emergency Appeal Fund, which provides full or partial underwriting for lifesaving care.

Off Manhattan Island

If you don't mind going out of town, there are several shelters of note in the greater metropolitan area: **ARF, The Animal Rescue Fund**, in Wainscott, New York, the **North Shore Animal League** in Port Washington, New York, and the **Saint Hubert's Giralda Animal Welfare and Education Center** in Madison, New Jersey.

ARF, The Animal Rescue Fund of the Hamptons, Inc., Daniel's Hole Road, P.O. Box 901, Wainscott, NY 11975, 516-537-0400, rescues and makes available for adoption homeless dogs. Pure and mixed breeds of all ages are available. They also offer low-cost spaying/neutering as well as referral and support services to new owners. ARF is open seven days a week from 1:00 to 4:00 P.M.

The North Shore Animal League, 25 Davis Avenue, Port Washington, NY 11050, 516-883-7575, is one of the largest shelters and adoption centers in the greater metropolitan area. North Shore is open from 9:00 A.M. to 9:00 P.M. (until 10:00 P.M. in the summer), and supplies adopted pets with a great accompaniment of support services. Spaying/neutering and thirty days of free veterinary care at their clinic are included with every adoption as well as free biweekly training classes. North Shore is a great option.

St. Hubert's Giralda, 575 Woodland Avenue, Madison, NJ 07940, 201-377-2295, is located on the grounds of the beautiful Dodge estate in Madison, New Jersey, about an hour out of Manhattan. They have strays and owner-surrendered dogs from the twelve surrounding towns. The shelter is open seven days a week from 12:00 until 4:00 P.M. There is a counselor evaluation for prospective "new parents," so be prepared for them to check references and call your landlord. A donation fee of $65 includes spaying or neutering. St. Hubert's Giralda has one of the best reputations of working for animals' welfare and raising the public's consciousness of animals' concerns. You can't go wrong with them.

Dog Rescue in New York

Say you find a dog wandering in the street and take it home. After exhaustive phone calling, you discover that: 1) Nobody is missing the pet; 2) no relative or neighbor wants the pet; and 3) the shelters are full or closed. Luckily, there are many grassroots organizations operating in New York City on behalf of abandoned or stray dogs. These groups work to rescue and place abused and homeless dogs in permanent situations. They oversee a network of foster homes to house the rescued dogs as well as providing necessary veterinary care, training, and support to the foster families.

Irene Smith, of **The Animal Rescue Network of East Harlem, Inc.,** 511 East 118th Street, New York, NY 10035, 212-860-7746, not only rescues, rehabilitates, and places stray, abandoned, or feral dogs (and cats), but is working within her area to build a model community action program offering animal rescue and humane control at the local level. By involving members of the neighborhood, Irene raises consciousness about responsible pet ownership, and through fund-raising efforts like the Discount Dog Laundry (see chapter four) gives low-income pet owners the chance to earn credits toward veterinary care for their own animals. Irene closely screens the dogs she places, and has the expertise and judgment to ensure that they will do well in their new homes. You can trust her.

You may have seen the dog rescue work of Chitra Besboroda

of **Sentient Creatures, Inc.,** P.O. Box 765, Cathedral Station, New York, NY 10025, 212-865-5998, on New York Public Access television. Chitra is a tireless defender of the silent plight of New York's many "junkyard" dogs, poor creatures that are chained or confined in back lots to guard cars or equipment. She regularly goes on "rounds" of these wretched places, bringing food and water to the creatures who languish under the most horrible circumstances. Often, Chitra and her volunteers are the only non-abusive humans these dogs have ever seen. Many "canine prisoners" she visits are literally catatonic from the abuse, neglect, and lack of affection, just as human victims of abuse would be. You'd be amazed at how forcefully the cruel owners challenge Chitra's right to bring some aid to the suffering animals. She is often assaulted verbally and physically for her efforts, and when she is able to rescue a dog, rehabilitate it, and place it for adoption, the owners sometimes challenge *her* in court.

Sentient Creatures always has dogs in need of good homes available for adoption.

The Animal Project is run by Miriam Reik, 212-222-5495. She coordinates a complex network of people in the city who serve as foster families for abandoned dogs. The Animal Project places ads for the animals it is trying to place, and screens potential homes. About one third of their dogs are simply given up by their owners, the others saved from life on the streets or euthanasia in the pound. The Animal Project is always looking for foster homes in New York City. Give them a call if you can help them out or are interested in adopting a dog from them.

Beingkind, Inc. has rescued and placed over five hundred dogs and cats in the past year. They work the same way, through foster homes, and always need assistance and support. You can reach Linda Cherney at **Beingkind, Inc.,** P.O. Box 20560, Park West Station, New York, NY, 10025, 212-781-4888.

The Pure-Breed Rescue Movement

Between 25 and 30 percent of the hundreds of thousands of dogs in pounds and shelters in America are purebreds. Dogs beautiful enough to win show ribbons, both pet-quality puppies and adults, are surrendered or abandoned by owners. The pure-breed rescue movement works to save these canine aristocrats and find them new homes.

The movement works this way: "Fanciers" of a certain breed of dog are always on the lookout in pounds and shelters for dogs of that particular breed. When they find one, they rescue it, saving it from a possible sad end. Necessary veterinary work is done, and behavioral problems are addressed.

Although adopters are asked to make a donation to defray the rescuer's costs, breed rescue is *not* a profit-making venture. The work goes on all over America, out of people's homes, and for only one reason—the love of the animals. If you're looking to adopt a purebred, a rescue group is an ideal source for healthy, well-mannered dogs.

I know of two Manhattanites, devoted members of a dachshund rescue, who are always ready to swoop in and rescue abused or abandoned dachshunds. When the demands of their hectic Wall Street careers interfere with this work, they simply hire a car service to pick up the dachshunds in distress.

That's panache!

There are rescue groups for every imaginable breed, from the Affenpinscher to the rare Xoloitzcuintli or Mexican hairless dog, but it took Shirley Weber at **PROJECT BREED, Inc.,** 187078 Curry Powder Lane, Germantown, MD 20874, for us to be able to find them.

After working at shelters in her native Maryland, she hooked into the rescue movement and started putting together directories of the various concerned groups in a given area. Several years and a vow of poverty later, she published the first *PROJECT BREED Directory*. Two editions of the directory now exist, containing listings and contacts for nearly 3,000 rescue groups serving 105 breeds of dog. The directories also include critiques of each breed, including advice on the pros and cons, health care, and upkeep of the different types. Invaluable references, the directories can be ordered for only $25. Get one!

If you are in a hurry to find a purebred dog through a rescue group, there is an angel in the city who can help you. **Robin Kovary,** 212-243-5460, is a dog trainer who has the directories and will refer you to the appropriate breed rescue groups. She is a wonderful dog-info source who will also give advice and guidance in your decision-making process.

Here are a few listings of phone numbers for pure-breed rescue groups, some with the contact people, in the northeast. There are *many* more, but this is a sampling:

Airedale Terrier Rescue & Adoption
203-431-6722

Alaskan Malamute Rescue & Adoption
203-649-0079

Boxer Rescue Service
Michelle McArdle, 203-853-9595;
Jean Loubriel, 201-768-6627

Bulldog Rescue
Barbara Mangini, 203-281-1409

Chinese Shar-Pei Rescue
Charlene Rogers, 203-747-6397

Dachshund Rescue
718-499-1934; 908-782-4724

Dalmatian Rescue
Carolyn Mullins, 203-421-4704

Yankee Golden Retriever Rescue, Inc.
twenty-four-hour hot line, 508-975-4091

Irish Setter Rescue & Adoption Network
Anna Jones, 908-464-5720

Labrador Retriever Rescue, Inc.
twenty-four-hour hot line, 508-369-8736

Newfoundland Rescue Service
Pat Macken, 609-265-9259;
Sandy Conklin, 201-779-8551

Pointer Rescue
Susan Tucker, 516-829-5327;
Erica Bandes, 203-266-7883

Pug Rescue of New England
Doris Aldrich, 413-253-3066

Scottish Terrier Club of Greater NY Rescue
William Berry, 201-227-1871

New England Shih Tzu Rescue
Bonnie Bean, 508-544-8808

Yankee Weimaraner Club Rescue & Adoption
Ellen O'Leske, 508-885-4255

It is important to remember that the pure-breed rescue movement is *not* based on the idea that purebreds are more worthy of rescue than mixed breeds. Rather, it's a way for people already knowledgeable about a particular breed to increase their volunteer efforts. Every purebred dog that moves onto the rescue underground railroad opens up space in a shelter for another homeless dog, thereby saving two dogs from euthanasia.

For those cruising the information highway, there is an e-mail discussion forum for dog rescue. Homeless pets from across the nation and Canada are posted by different rescue groups. Information is exchanged, and new homes found. To subscribe to the **Dog Rescue List,** send e-mail to "majordomo@netcom.com". Put nothing in the subject line; on the first line of the message, type, "subscribe dog-rescue" and your e-mail address. Delete your sig file, or anything else appearing in the body of the e-mail. Be prepared for many heartrending stories of abandoned dogs, but also a feeling that you are a part of something that is helping dogs in need.

The Beautiful Greyhounds

One really special pure-breed rescue movement attempts to save retired racing greyhounds. These elegant creatures are usually executed when their racing days are over. Thousands of young, healthy dogs are killed each year. Several organizations work to persuade the race owners or trainers to give them the unwanted dogs; they then place the animals in permanent homes.

Racing greyhounds are unique dogs who make *excellent* pets. There is some work to be done in introducing a racing animal to life at home, since at the track their lives are strictly regimented. Usually kept in crates or small pens on shredded newspaper in single-story kennel buildings, their days consist of walking on a leash to the track, racing, and returning to the kennel. Stairs, windows, and free interaction with other dogs (among other things) are foreign to them. The greyhound is not an aggressive breed, and actually is well suited to a New Yorker's lifestyle. They have gentle, responsive natures, having learned at the track to be dependent on and bonded to people. They thrive on personal attention and love.

All the greyhound owners I know have fond stories of introducing their dogs to "life on the outside." *CBS News* producer Lucy Scott lives in Manhattan with her retired racing greyhound,

Annie. "When I got Annie," she told me, "I had to teach her how to play. Imagine a two-year-old dog that had never played! I spent a lot of time pantomiming dog play to her, down on my hands and knees mimicking what I'd seen dogs do. She must have thought I was nuts, but she caught on! Now I have to drag her away from her play group in the park."

If you are interested in adopting a racing greyhound, you have a few choices. Lucy got Annie from **REGAP (Retired Greyhounds As Pets) of Connecticut Inc.,** P.O. Box 76, Bethany, CT 06524, 203-393-1673. They get dogs from different tracks and place them in new homes. REGAP has a retirement home/interim facility where dogs "detox" from the stress of track life before they are placed, and where older, infirm dogs can stay permanently. To their credit, the home is supported by the Plainfield Greyhound Park and individual kennel owners who are concerned for the welfare of the dogs after the races are over.

Should you decide that a retired racing dog would fit your

Lucy Scott and her retired racing greyhound, Annie, enjoying a beautiful day in Central Park by the Bethesda Fountain. Credit: Christine Butler

lifestyle, you can contact REGAP. There is a screening process, and a tax-deductible contribution of around $100.

Another greyhound adoption service is **Greyhound Friends Inc.**, 167 Saddle Hill Road, Hopkinton, MA 01748, 508-435-5969. They also save racing greyhounds given to them by owners and trainers at various New England tracks. The donation fee is about $75, and like REGAP, they will give you plenty of information and support as you introduce your new pet to life off the track.

Guide Dog and Service Dog Schools

Many institutions raise and train dogs to serve people who are physically or visually challenged, and these schools can be an excellent source for your dream dog. Guide dog schools usually own their own breeding colonies of goldens, Labs, and sometimes German shepherds.

Guiding Eyes for the Blind Breeding Center, P.O. Box 228-A, Rt. 164, Patterson, NY 12563, 914-878-3330, frequently has excellent golden retriever, Labrador, and German shepherd puppies available. Often pups are too big, or don't fit within the exacting temperament guidelines that would make them suitable guides. Also, dogs who "wash out" of the difficult guide training are offered for adoption. If you are looking to get a golden, Lab, or shepherd, call this source first!

NEADS, The National Education of Assistance Dog Service, West Boylston, MA 01583, 508-835-3304, trains dogs to live with and assist deaf or hearing-impaired people, as well as people confined to wheelchairs. To assist the hearing-impaired they use smaller dogs, who display keen listening and communicative skills. The dogs are taken into the program and trained to act as the "ears" for a human companion by alerting him or her to the doorbell, alarm clock, and a host of other auditory cues. Bigger breeds such as labs and goldens are trained to aid the wheelchair-bound. They serve their owners by doing everything from retrieving keys and other items to turning on lights and helping them get around. As with guide dogs, sometimes partially trained dogs also "wash out" of the program and are available for adoption as pets. Call them for more information if you're interested.

If you pick up a dog and make him prosperous, he will not bite you. This is the principal difference between a dog and a man.

—Mark Twain

Pet Stores

I'd like to talk briefly about buying your puppy from a pet store. Most people concerned with the rights and welfare of animals oppose selling dogs as retail merchandise. No matter what the pet store tells you, the puppies it offers frequently come from poor-quality breeders, commonly known as "puppy mills." Legally, they can call themselves breeders, and their dogs are *always* registered with the AKC to make them seem more legitimate. In truth, they are usually substandard kennels where dogs are kept for the sole purpose of reproduction. The puppies are more likely to have congenital problems, and poor health, than puppies from a reputable breeder. A responsible breeder cares about his dogs. He wants to meet and screen potential owners, and is unlikely to sell pups to a shop where they will be hawked as merchandise. Puppy mills/breeders who supply pet stores aren't interested in what happens to their babies. The profit margin, *not* the well-being of the animal, is their main concern.

Notice how the cutest puppies are *always* displayed in the pet shop window to catch your eye as you pass on the street? These shops anticipate that you will be overcome by the "How much is that doggie in the window?" syndrome. But remember, that emotive rush of "Ooooh, lookit the puppy!" is *not* the best reason to buy a dog. *Of course they're cute, they're puppies!* Remember, you are assuming a ten- to fifteen-year responsibility—don't make such a serious decision on a whim. Those who work in animal rescue and in shelters see a *high percentage* of "impulse buys" surrendered or abandoned. When the pup gets older and requires training or develops bad habits, the positive "Oooh, lookit the puppy" vibe is gone, and the dog is given away.

Since pet shop puppies are often "impulse buys," you will see pups of a particularly "chic" breed marked up astronomically, while less trendy or older puppies are discounted. Walk into the back of the store and notice the four- and five-month-olds who haven't been sold. Grown out of their "cutesy window display stage," these canine adolescents should be getting exercise and socialization. A breeder with older pups begins basic training and gets them out and about, because developmentally, that's what the dogs need. These guys are stuck in cages or small runs, waiting for someone to buy them so that their lives can begin.

Pet stores are in the business of selling puppies for profit. Where the pups come from, who buys them, and what happens to the dogs after the sale are not their concerns. This is not to say that the *individual pups* themselves are to blame. They are innocent creatures, and to be fair, I know of several sweet, relatively healthy dogs who came from New York pet stores. But I echo the sentiments of many dog lovers when I say that dogs *deserve more* than to be treated as retail merchandise.

Know Your Rights When You Buy!

Let's talk about what protection the dog-buying consumer has under New York state law. These laws apply to "pet dealers," including most breeders, and pet shops selling dogs, but *not* to humane societies and shelters or not-for-profit guide schools.

Article 35-B of New York State Business Law sets forth certain rights of the consumer:

> *Within fourteen days of the sale of a dog or cat, the consumer has the right to take the animal to a licensed veterinarian of his or her choice, and should the vet find the animal unfit, due to illness, congenital malformation, or symptoms of a disease, the "pet dealer" must offer the consumer some options:*
>
>   *A) returning the animal, and receiving a refund for the sale price, and reasonable veterinary costs;*
>
>   *B) returning the animal, and taking a replacement pet of the consumer's choice, and restitution for the vet bills of the first animal;*
>
>   *C) or the right to keep the sick animal, and be*

A really companionable and indispensable dog is an accident of nature. You can't get it by breeding for it and you can't buy it with money. It just happens along. Out of the vast sea of assorted dogs that I have had dealings with, by far the noblest, the best, the most important was the first. . . . He was an old-style collie, beautifully marked, with a blunt nose, and a great natural gentleness and intelligence. When I got him he was what I badly needed. I think probably all these other dogs of mine have been just a groping toward that old dream. I've never dared get another collie for fear the comparison would be too uncomfortable. I can still see my first dog in all the moods and situations that memory has filed him away in, but I think of him oftenest as he used to be right after breakfast on the back porch, listlessly eating up a dish of petrified oatmeal rather than hurt my feelings. For six years he met me at the same place after school, and conveyed me home, a service he thought up himself. A boy doesn't forget that sort of association. It is a monstrous trick of fate that now, settled in the country and with sheep to take care of, I am obliged to do my shepherding with the grotesque and sometimes underhanded assistance of two dachshunds and a wirehaired fox terrier.

—E. B. White

reimbursed for veterinary services from a licensed vet of the consumer's choosing, for curing, or trying to cure, the sick animal. The reimbursement of the last option must not exceed the original purchase price.

Again, this only applies to breeders and pet stores or other "pet vendors" in New York State, but at least it affords the consumer some protection.

Frequently, a breeder or pet store will offer a written

"health guarantee" with a puppy. Usually, these documents offer the purchaser the rights already assured by state law. Health guarantees can be helpful in states without consumer protection laws, but "guaranteeing" a living creature is a tricky business.

Obviously, it's wrong to sell you a sick puppy, but sometimes the maladies which the breeder "guarantees" against don't show up for a year or so. By this time you are emotionally involved with your pet. Even if the breeder has "guaranteed" to replace a dog with problems, you may decide to keep the pet you love and treat the ailments rather than returning him to the breeder (where he may be euthanized) and taking a replacement puppy. Remember, the replacement pup from the breeder will probably be from *the same bloodlines as the first dog,* so you could be looking at the identical situation a year down the road.

Hip Dysplasia? OFA? What?

Hip dysplasia is a crippling, genetic condition causing lameness and severe arthritis. Thanks to irresponsible breeding practices, it now exists in almost every mid- to large-sized breed of dog. Because hip dysplasia usually doesn't show up until the dog is mature, the only way to screen for it is by having an X ray taken of the dog's hip joints when he is at least a year old. You may send the films to the **Dysplasia Control Registry** at the **Orthopedic Foundation for Animals (OFA),** 2300 Nifong Boulevard, Columbia, MO 65201, 314-442-0418, where a specialist will examine the radiographs and evaluate how "correct"—or likely to develop dysplasia—the dog is. A responsible breeder will check any dogs she plans to use for breeding and will only mate those free of problems.

If you are buying a puppy from a breed subject to hip dysplasia (Akitas, Bernese mountain dogs, rotties, Labs, goldens, and shepherds especially!), the breeder should include, with the pedigree, the OFA registry numbers of both parents—and grandparents! If the parents of your prospective puppy were screened and found to be free of this crippling condition, they are unlikely to pass it on to their offspring.

Finding a Breeder

The best thing to do is to choose a breeder wisely. The dogs should be registered with one of the major all-breed registries, like the AKC or the UKC, and the breeder should supply you with the necessary paperwork so that you can register your puppy as well. If the puppy cannot be registered, the breeder should be forthcoming with an explanation, and you *should not* be paying full price since you have no way of verifying the pup's parentage or entering him in competitions sanctioned by the registries. Remember, though, being registered is *not* a guarantee of good health or temperament; it simply means that the pup's lineage can be traced.

The breeder should also have taken the puppies to a licensed veterinarian for an examination and their first and sometimes second set of shots at six and eight weeks *before* you pick up your pup. You will be responsible for the next series of shots at eleven and fourteen weeks.

Beware of those turning out a lot of puppies—quality control usually suffers. Beware of breeders "guaranteeing" you the moon and the stars. Honest breeders stand behind their puppies absolutely. They love their breed bitches and think of their offspring as practically family. Familiarize yourself with the common health problems of the breed you are considering so that you can ask informed questions. For instance, hip dysplasia is so common in German shepherds that if you run across a breeder who swears they've never seen it in their dogs, it had better be their first litter; otherwise, they've got a credibility problem. Instead, ask what the tendencies are in the bloodlines, and how the breeder is working to minimize problems. Are they breeding with the aim of cloning their one champion show dog, or producing puppies with good health, brains, and temperaments? The most an honest breeder can do is breed the best to the best and hope for the proverbial best. Genetics is still, at best, a roll of the DNA dice.

So, you've heard my cautionary tale, and you still want a warm, wiggly bundle of love to light up your life. What to do? A good way to find a breeder is to observe a dog you really like in the park, on the street, at your vet's office—wherever—and ask the owner where he or she got the dog. Sounds simple, I know, but why not? Believe me, nothing makes a New York dog owner prouder than the chance to wax poetic on the wonders of his or her dog and direct others to the same breeder—the source of all the joy.

Friends Jean Blanchard and Susan Gaffney live in the same building and their Havanese and Bolognese dogs play together. Both are rare breeds, representing two of the four family branches of the original Mediterranean dogs, the other two being the better known Maltese and bichon frise. The Havanese traveled with the Spanish aristocracy to the Caribbean, where they were so prized that they could only be given as gifts, not sold for money. Both breeds make clever, sturdy companions, merry playmates, and excellent watchdogs—in short, wonderful choices for your New York dog. Credit: Petography

Since this *is* New York, once a year we have the most important dog show in the nation in our backyard. Go to Westminster—Madison Square Garden, the second week of February—or to other dog shows, and talk to breeders. Ask your vet for suggestions. If you want one of the breeds used for guide work, call some of the guide dog schools previously mentioned. Even if they breed their own dogs, they are getting new stock from somewhere and can often refer you to a good breeder.

The **American Kennel Club**'s 1-900-407-7877 (PUPS) is a service that can help. If you call them during business hours, give them your location and breed of choice. They will refer you to the secretaries of breed specialty clubs (made up of breeders) in your area. The secretaries usually know which club members have puppies and can direct you to your dream baby.

DOGS U.S.A. (P.O. Box 55811, Boulder, CO 80322) is a giant breeder directory that also includes stories and articles on caring for your pup. It is also available at many city newsstands and at most Petland Discounts stores.

The classified sections of *Dog World* and *Dog Fancy* magazines, which you can find in most magazine shops, contain splashy advertisements by breeders all over the country. They have pictures and promises and are a lot of fun to look at, as well as being pretty informative. Remember, though, that *Dog Fancy* also prints a *disclaimer* disavowing any implied endorsement of particular breeders.

Finding your puppy or adult dog is, of course, just the beginning. Now starts the grand adventure that is life in New York with a dog.

Chapter 2

Walking the New York Dog

*There is no doubt that every healthy, normal boy
(if there is such a thing in these days of Child
Study) should own a dog at some time in his life,
preferably between the ages of forty-five and fifty.*
—**Robert Benchley**

A few hours after you bring your new dog home—or a few minutes if it's a puppy—you realize that your schedule has changed forever. This dog is going to need to go outside, and regularly! If you hadn't *already* memorized how many stairs made up a flight in your walk-up, or the names of all the city inspectors who have dutifully come by, inspected the elevator, and signed the posted certificate, you will now. Actually, elevator certificates can make interesting reading. I have noticed that ex-presidents and rock stars frequently moonlight as elevator inspectors in New York.

In chapter five I discuss services you can hire for your dog, including professional "dog walkers." These full-time canine pals will come to your house once or twice a day and take your dog out for half an hour or so. It is a wonderful way to arrange exercise and "airing" for your pet when your busy lifestyle keeps you away from home.

To avoid trips outside, many New Yorkers have trained their dogs to relieve themselves in the apartment on papers or "Wee Wee Pads" (picture a disposable diaper, but flat). I have even heard of dogs who use cat litter box setups or avail themselves of the bathtub. I assume that this would work better with the smaller breeds—but who knows—it's a big town, and anything is possible.

A List of Dog Dangers Before You Venture Forth

ELEVATOR DOORS

I know it sounds impossible, but many New York dogs have been injured, and even killed, when the ends of their leashes caught in closed elevator doors. This can happen *anytime* you get in an elevator with your dog. Classically, you're going out with your dog, you snap the leash on before you leave the apartment, and you go down the hall to wait for the elevator. It comes, you and

New York City's Police and Transit Dogs

Canines are hard at work every day in New York City, helping police and transit officers. There are several different canine units. German shepherds are used by the NYPD and transit police for patrol work, apprehension of suspects, evidence retrieval, tracking, and building or area searches. Labrador retrievers are used by the bomb and arson divisions to identify and locate explosives or traces of flammable materials that would indicate that a fire was set deliberately. The NYPD's Special Operations Division Canine Program uses shepherds and the grand old man of scent discrimination, the bloodhound, for especially challenging tracking and missing-persons assignments.

The dogs generally live with their human partners, joining their families, so that a deep and lasting relationship forms. The better the dog and handler know each other and the more they trust each other, the better they will work together. After a dog is retired, he continues to live with his officer, and if the officer retires or is transferred or promoted, his dog retires and continues to live with him as a pet.

your dog step on, and as you reach to press the button, you drop the leash. The end of the leash falls outside the door, which closes on it. The elevator starts to go down, and your dog goes up. You must have the presence of mind to *instantly* unsnap the leash from the collar. If the leash is attached to the "choke" ring or to a spiked collar, you might have a dead dog.

This is no joke. A friend of a friend of mine got off the elevator in the lobby of her building. Her Tibetan terrier lingered in the elevator, greeting a pug who got on in the lobby. The terrier's owner stopped and called her dog, who scooted out after her through the closing door. But the terrier's dragging leash was closed in the door. As the elevator went up, so did the terrier. The owner grabbed her ascending dog and, thankfully, her weight was enough to break the leather collar the terrier was wearing. When it broke, she lost her balance and crashed down on the lobby marble, her dog safe in her arms. The terrier was okay, but the owner severely injured her knees in the fall.

ESCALATORS

This would seem obvious, but many a New York pooch has come to grief by not stepping cleanly off an escalator. Remember, escalator savvy is an element of the training a guide or service dog undergoes. How would a dog know that the steps are going to disappear? This happened in a famous department store to my girlfriend's poodle, Coco Chanel. Marci was carrying Coco when they stepped on the escalator, but Coco started fussing, so she put her down. As the steps collapsed, Coco didn't know to *step up*, and those awful metal teeth caught her front paws. Coco screamed bloody murder, my girlfriend screamed in horror, and then snatched her out of the machine. They rushed to the veterinarian, where Coco's mangled front paws were treated and sewn up. The paws eventually healed, but even today, the nails on Coco's front paws point in all different directions. Unless you have trained your dog to step cleanly off the escalator, do *not* let him or her stand and ride up.

POISONS

In an attempt to keep the New York City vermin population to a minimum, the Parks Department routinely places poisoned rat bait around city parks. They always post signs warning that the area is baited and try to bury the bait, but strong rains, and digging dogs, bring the poison to the surface. DON'T let your dog eat, or dig anything up, in the parks! If you even suspect that he has ingested some rat poison, call your vet or the **National Animal Poison Control Center,** 800-548-2423.

Although it seems harmless, automobile antifreeze is incredibly toxic to dogs. To make matters worse, the sweet smell and taste of antifreeze attracts canines, but ingesting as little as a tablespoon of it can prove fatal. Be aware of any suspicious yellow puddles by the curb where someone may have changed their antifreeze or where it may have leaked from a car. If your dog licks any of it up, immediately call your vet or the **Poison Control Center.**

Thus forewarned, you may venture forth.

Walking your New York dog is a daily ritual. As far as schedule goes, most people do a long early morning walk, a long just-home-from-work walk, and a quick 'round the block walk before bed. An evening stroll is often added—particularly in lovely weather.

Of course puppies need to go out much more frequently. If you have a puppy, you will be keenly involved in house-training. Meeting his bathroom needs in a positive, constructive way will have become a science in your house. You will be calculating his digestive patterns, sleep cycle, and excitement level and orchestrating them with getting him outside, thus keeping the "accidents" to a minimum.

In training a recently city-transplanted country dog, the process can be a little tricky as well. New York City is almost completely paved. It's the proverbial asphalt jungle, and your dog may insist on feeling grass and leaves beneath his paws for his system to work. This will change. City dogs learn to use the curb by necessity, but even in the heart of the metropolis there is some turf to be found. You just have to know where to look, and observe a few rules.

Canine Leash and Sanitation Laws

The city of New York strictly enforces the leash and clean-up law. All dogs must be leashed, and you must pick up and dispose of his/her waste. Legally, dogs may be off the leash only while inside one of New York's five fenced "dog runs." There is a general feeling that the leash law is *not* enforced before 8:00 or 9:00 A.M. While this may be the case, and it might be unlikely for you to be ticketed at your morning dog group, there is no law supporting it. The regulations are very clear—no dogs off the leash, period (see chapter ten).

Remember, any city "officer"—sanitation officer, police officer, or parks enforcement officer—has the authority to write a summons fining the owner of an unleashed or un-picked-up-after dog up to $250. Don't think they can't just because they often choose not to enforce the law. If they catch you, and decide to write a summons, it is not a joke, and insulting their intelligence, pretending you never saw your dog before, or crying only makes matters worse. If you have no ID and they suspect that you have given them a bogus name and address, they may escort you home to get your ID. These summonses and violations are serious, and I don't recommend that you try the argument "Shouldn't you be chasing *real* criminals, not me and my dog?" Just apologize, pay your fine, and observe the laws.

This may seem confining, but imagine New York City *without* a clean-up law (have you been to Paris lately?). And the leash law is as much for your dog's protection as anything else.

Unleashed dogs are often hit by cars. Just last month a dalmatian I frequently see in the park was hit. The owner felt that Domino the dalmatian was so well trained that he would respond to his slightest command, and often let the dog off the leash. A dog may indeed be well trained, but as an even cursory glance at any day's headlines will tell you, there is no way to predict what can happen in New York. Sure enough, one day a loud noise from a construction site frightened Domino and he leapt blindly into the traffic on Central Park West. He was hit, and rolled under a cab. In pain and confusion, he ran into the park, disappearing into the Ramble. Domino was lucky, he only had a broken leg, and was subsequently found. Amazingly enough, I saw the pair a week later, Domino off the leash *again*, hobbling along with his leg in a cast. Some people just don't get it.

It's impossible to anticipate what dogs will encounter in Manhattan, so for their own safety, keep them leashed.

Dog Runs

The only way to give your dog a chance to run off the leash is to visit one of the legal dog runs. A dog run is a fenced free play area to be enjoyed by all. Of course, basic "dog run etiquette"

Why Do Dogs Always Want to Be with Us?

Are you amazed by your dog's unfailing wish to be by your side or within sight of you? Is it because you are a fascinating conversationalist? Not exactly.

The loyalty of dogs is a deep instinct. Yes, they love you and enjoy your company, but the profound need to be with you comes directly from their wolf ancestry.

The only stability in the life of the wolf is the pack he belongs to. Members of the pack work together to survive. It takes the concerted full-time efforts of all the adults in the company to hunt and kill enough game to support the pack. To enjoy the luxury of a semipermanent residence in a den, the pack must find an area with enough available game for the hunting members to go out daily and bring food back for the others. If the prey disappears, then the pack must move on to find better hunting elsewhere.

Because a wolf is dependent on the pack for survival, separation from them can spell disaster for the individual. Once separated, there is no way for an individual to be sure where the others have gone, since the pack must follow the game they hunt. If detached from its pack, a wolf faces survival on its own. Staying with the pack is everything.

You represent your dog's adopted pack. You provide him with the food and emotional security that the pack would. It is genetically coded in him, from his wolf ancestors, to stay with his pack—you. Of course, dogs learn from experience that when you go away to work or leave for a vacation, you eventually come back. Still, there remains enough of the wolf instinct in the domesticated dog that his impulse will always be to go with you. This is one of the many reasons that the life of the working guide dog or the police dog is so fulfilling; they are allowed to go with their pack—their human partners—at all times.

So the next time your dog leaps up in alarm from a deep sleep when he senses that you are reaching for your overcoat, don't chastise him. Explain patiently for the kagillionth time that dogs are not allowed in the supermarket. Better yet, do all your shopping at the Korean grocery, where your dog can sneak in with you!

(or common sense) applies. Before you enter the run, check out the dogs already present. Are they well matched in size and temperament to yours? Your dog may be perfectly friendly, but might she overwhelm, or be overwhelmed by, others in the run? Take a moment to assess the situation.

All dogs should be current with their vaccinations and worm-free. Aggressive dogs or bitches in heat should only enter the run if it's vacant. Clean up after your dog, and continue to supervise her behavior. Obnoxious barking, even in play, will annoy the neighbors, and if it occurs before 9:00 A.M. or after 9:00 P.M., the noise could be grounds to close the run.

Above all, do not use the dog run as a free doggie baby-sitter. Don't drop your dog off for an hour of play while you shop. Leaving your dog is inconsiderate, irresponsible, and dangerous. You are responsible for your dog's actions at all times. If that is not enough, remember that many dogs have been stolen out of runs.

Currently there are several fenced dog runs in Manhattan, recognized by the city's Department of Parks and Recreation, and several other non-Parks Department runs. The Parks Department has none in the other boroughs. Here are the Manhattan locations:

West Side

•Riverside Park: near the promenade at West 86th Street, and inside the 103rd Street entrance

•Museum Park: 81st Street and Columbus Avenue

East Side

•Carl Schurz Park: south slope side of the 86th Street mall

Downtown

•Washington Square Park: "George's Run," south side

•Tompkins Square Park: east end corner

•Pearl Street Dog Run: corner of Pearl and Dover streets

Uptown

•J. Hood Wright Park: west side

As I write this, a Madison Square Park dog run is in the works. For continuing information on dog runs in Manhattan, you can call the **Manhattan Borough Office of the Department of Parks and Recreation,** 212-408-0212, 16 West 61st Street, New York, NY 10023.

If you are interested in securing a dog run in your neighborhood, the best thing to do is to form a "Friends of _____ Park Dog Run" group (for examples, see the "Pro-Dog City Groups" section on the next page) with like-minded dog owners in your area, and begin the exhausting, very political process of bringing a proposal for a dog run before your local community board. It takes persistence, but if you succeed, you'll have won a prize your dog can enjoy every day.

Alternative Runs

There are some "less official" options. Informal dog runs exist all over the city. They include the 11th Street playground in the West Village, P.S. 51's playground (West 44th Street between 10th and 11th avenues), on Hudson Street, and in Battery Park City (the corner of West Thames and Little West streets). Of course, Manhattan dogs avail themselves of many school yards and empty lots, and the best thing to do is ask around at your local pet shop or vet's office for neighborhood "resources."

Downtown, on Mercer Street, across from the Angelica Film Center Theater, there is a private dog run supervised by the **Mercer-Houston Dog Run Association, Inc.,** 532 LaGuardia Place, Suite 485, New York, NY 10021, 212-505-0304. It's for members only, and for a $50 yearly fee, you get a key to the locked yard. Of course, since it is member maintained, you must clean up after your dog and follow a strict set of rules. There is a waiting list for run privileges, and it can take as long as six months before you and your dog are accepted.

I have a friend whose dog, Scout, spent more than six months on the waiting list for the Mercer-Houston run. Finally, in desperation, he started shamelessly name dropping—hinting that Scout was the bastard offspring of one of William Wegman's dogs! When the acceptance letter finally arrived in the mail, he felt as though Scout had gotten into Harvard.

Pro-Dog City Groups

Dog runs being summarily closed is a recurring problem on the island of Manhattan, but sometimes progress can come out of what seems like disaster. The J. J. Walker Park in the West Village had been a popular unofficial run, but when plans were made to renovate the park, the needs of the local dog community were not considered by the city. Without warning, one morning the park was locked. Adding insult to injury, a policeman was issuing no trespassing violations to owners who disregarded the fence. This was a little too much for neighborhood residents Tracey and Randy Sides. Ably assisted by their dog, Zach, the Sides founded the **West Village Dog Owner's Group (DOG),** 41 Bethune Street, New York, NY 10014, dedicated to "improving the quality of life for dogs in Manhattan."

In response to the loss of their local run in the West Village, DOG has planned a gorgeous new private run on Pier 52 in the West Village. They hope that it will span two-thirds of an acre with trees, a swimming pool, and a separate section for small dogs and puppies. A membership fee of $50 a year is anticipated to pay for upkeep and a part-time caretaker. Membership for this model run will be kept to five hundred, so if you live anywhere within walking distance, contact them!

West Village DOG intends to turn their energies to the rest of the island. They want to put forth the concerns of dog owners so that the city accommodates our needs in all park planning.

Other similar groups in Manhattan are **Friends of Madison Square Park,** P.O. Box 2924, Grand Central Station, New York, NY 10163, organized to promote a dog run in the park, and **Friends of Museum Park Dog Run,** 15 West 81st Street, New York, NY 10024.

Brooklyn has two similar groups working to support dog owners. **The Brooklyn Heights Dog Owners Association,** 212-387-2011, sponsors activities and events and offers member discounts with participating neighborhood merchants. The newly formed **Prospect Park Dog Outreach Group,** 445 17th Street, Apt. 4, Brooklyn, NY 11215, 718-499-4145, is trying to extend off-leash times for dogs in Prospect Park, as well as other community-oriented services.

The Parks

New York City's parks are the most obvious playground for city dogs. If you live near one, you're probably familiar with the "dog culture" by now. Social "play groups" congregate daily in the same area, at about the same time. The dogs socialize and play while the owners stand around watching them, talking. As informal and fluid as this is, it's a culture unto itself.

There are play groups near almost every park entrance from about 6:30 A.M. until 10:30 A.M., and again in the afternoon from 4:00 P.M. until dark. Inside Central Park, the Great Lawn and the ball fields sport some serious dog groups. Usually, your schedule will coincide with one or more of the groups.

A basenji-owning friend of mine has a theory that there is really only one dog group and that the rest revolve in parallel universes. Strange though it sounds, every dog group does seem to have about four frisbee-focused golden retrievers in various hues, a new Lab puppy, a six-month-old dalmatian or wiemaraner bitch, a few mixed breeds, a beagle, a pug, and a brace of some kind of terrier. You can wander into a new dog group and experience a profound sense of déjà vu.

In the broader context, there is without question a doggie parallel universe coexisting with the rest of New York City life. A canine on the end of your leash is the instant entrée into this doggie world. You and your dog will be greeted, accepted, and included by both dogs and their owners. If you wish, you'll establish an entire support system of dog friends. One word of warning: Don't be offended if everyone remembers your dog's name and not yours!

If you *do* walk your dog in Central Park, don't miss the statue of the **Sled Dog Balto** (about 50 yards inside the park if you enter on Fifth Avenue at East 67th Street). The bronze sculpture of the noble dog is dedicated to "the indomitable spirit of the Sled Dog . . . " and tells the story of the lifesaving trip that brought medicine to the people of Nome, Alaska, in the winter of 1925. This heroic journey is memorialized every year in the running of the famous Iditarod dogsled race.

A little farther inside the park, by the ball fields, is the **Central Park Carousel**, which offers rides to New York dogs and their owners—*if* they sit in either of the two chariots, *not* on the carousel horses. There is a famous story, heard on National Public Radio, about a successful Japanese restaurateur who had an Akita named Kita. Kita became enamored of the carousel, having spent his puppyhood in Japan where they don't have such contraptions, and would gaze at it dreamily as he passed on his daily walk. On a lark one day, his owner bought him a ride. They sat formally in the chariot, going around and around. Well, that was *it*! From that day forward, Kita refused to pass the carousel without a ride. Kita's daily spin in the chariot became a fixture, and is remembered fondly to this day by those who run it.

In Brooklyn Heights, "Squib Hill," located at Columbia Heights and Vine Street, is one of the most popular places for morning and evening dog gatherings. The Jehovah's Witnesses own it and keep the grounds in beautiful shape—so be extra careful to pick up after your pet!

Prospect Park offers Brooklyners a gorgeous dog outlet, complete with ponds and streams for splashing in, and the Great Meadow for ball chasing and playing.

Jacob Riis Park, in Brooklyn, actually has a beach that city dogs can enjoy in the off-season (before Memorial Day and after Labor Day).

The Bronx boasts Van Cortlandt Park, with beautiful meadows, woods, picnic areas, and ball fields. Van Cortlandt Urban Park Rangers, 212-548-7070, can provide guided tours or will steer you toward some of the park's wonderful hiking trails.

Wherever you go in New York City, there is no more pleasant way to break the ice with other New Yorkers than to have a dog. This was documented in a roundabout manner when the *Village Voice* cited the Upper West Side dog run by the Museum of Natural History as "the hottest new spot to meet people" (I am loath to say "pick up"). I guess in the seventies it was singles bars, in the eighties it was the health club scene, and now for the nineties we have the dog runs. At least with this approach you are guaranteed a rewarding, fulfilling relationship—with your dog!

So get out there, and walk that dog!

On your excursions, be sure to offer your pooch a drink of water. **The Pet Travel Canteen,** from **Oasis Pet Products,** 2242 Davis Court, Hayward, CA 94545, available at **Karen's for People and Pets,** 1195 Lexington Avenue, New York, NY 10028, 212-472-9440, and at **Pet Necessities,** 236 East 75th

Some of the Most Aptly Named New York Dogs

A wire (haired) fox terrier, named Hairbrush
A Great Pyrenees, belonging to a psychiatrist, named Ego
A komondor with her dread-locked coat, named Schmatta

Street, New York, NY, 10021, 212-988-0769, is a combination canteen and bowl that holds a quart. Fill it up before you go out, and you can give your dog a little refreshment along the way.

If you have a little guy with legs that become fatigued after many crosstown blocks, why not carry him in a Pac A Pet? **Pac A Pet,** from **JB Associates,** Department DF, P.O. Box 1045, Boise, ID 83701, 208-853-5845, is a nylon backpack of sorts, which may be worn in the front and has a safety leash inside. It is designed for small dogs to ride in comfort and is available with a removable fleece liner for the winter, an extra pillow, and comes in two sizes. Small, for dogs under eight pounds, and large, for dogs up to fourteen pounds.

Need your hands free for shopping? **Alpine Pet,** 955 Massachusetts Avenue, Ste. 314, Department F, Cambridge, MA 02139, 800-424-7463, has a "Sporting Lead," an over-the-shoulder dog leash. Available in three adjustable sizes in either bridle leather or nylon, it accommodates up to two dogs. You wear the leash across your torso, leaving your hands free to push a stroller or carry a giant Bloomies shopping bag.

Frequently, Serena and I spend a Saturday morning exploring neighborhoods beyond our own. A particular favorite is Ninth Avenue between 34th Street and the mid-Forties. The home of many distinctive international food shops, this area is a pleasure to visit with your dog, since so many of the shopkeepers keep the "old world values"—and welcome your dog inside! Of course you must be careful that your pet doesn't bother the other customers and keeps his nose to himself, away from the freshly baked bread or the delicious cheeses!

If you live on the east side, a wonderful area to walk your dog is the promenade that runs along the East River. You can easily get access to this by walking east on 63rd Street to the overpass that crosses FDR Drive. (On your way, you might want to stop at the **Sutton Dog Parlor's Doggie Deli** on East 60th

from "The Thin Red Leash"

It takes courage for a tall thin man to lead a tiny Scotch terrier pup on a smart red leash in our neighborhood, that region bounded roughly (and how!) by Hudson and West Streets, where the Village takes off its Windsor tie and dons its stevedore corduroys. Here men are guys and all dogs are part bull. Here "cute" apartments stand quivering like pioneers on the prairie edge.

The first day that I sallied forth with Black Watch III bounding tinily at the end of the thin red leash, a cement finisher, one of the crowd that finds an esoteric pleasure in standing on the bleak corner of Hudson and Horatio Streets, sat down on the sidewalk and guffawed. There were hoots and whistles.

It was apparent that the staunch and plucky Scotch terrier breed was, to these uninitiated bulldog-lovers, the same as a Pekinese. But Black Watch must have his airing. So I continued to brave such witticisms as "Hey, fella, where's the rest of it?" and—this from a huge steamfitter—"What d'y' say me an' you an' the dog go somewheres and have tea?". . .

. . . The following evening the gang was more numerous than ever. A gigantic chap lunged forward at us. He had the build of a smokestack-wrecker.

"Psst!" he hissed. Black Watch held his ground.

"They're scrappers, these dogs," I protested amiably.

"What d'they scrap—cockroaches?" asked another man among general laughter. I realized that now was the time to die. After all, there are certain slurs that you can't take about your dog. Just then a monstrous man, evidently a former Hudson Duster who lifts locomotives from track to track when the turntables are out of order, lunged out of a doorway.

"Whadda we got here?" he growled.

"Park Avenue Pooch," sneered one. The train-lifter eyed Black Watch, who was wagging his tail in a most friendly manner.

"Scottie, ain't it?" asked the train-lifter, producing a sack of scrap tobacco.

"Yeah," I said as easily as I could.

"Damn fine dogs, Scotties," said the train-lifter. "You gotta good'un here, when it puts on some age, scout. Hellcats in a fight, too, I mean. Seen one take the tonsil out of a Airedale one day."

"Yeah?" asked the smokestack-wrecker.

"Yeah," said the train-lifter.

"Yeah," said I.

. . . We're quite good friends now, Black Watch and the gang and I. They call him Blacki. I am grateful to a kind of fate that had given the train-lifter the chance, between carrying locomotives, to see a Scottie in action.

—*James Thurber*

Street, between Second and First avenues, for a quick dog treat!). Once over the FDR, a beautiful promenade snakes along the river, offering views of Roosevelt Island, the swirling water, and the underside of some of Manhattan's most exclusive apartments.

On the promenade, keep your dog leashed. Although it is fenced, there are breaks in the barrier on the river side where boats dock. Many an excited dog has jumped or fallen into the water, frequently with disastrous consequences. To make matters worse, owners dive into the river to rescue their pets—again, with sometimes tragic consequences. Please exercise an ounce of prevention and keep the leashes on.

The problem of "suddenly swimming dogs" is also an issue at the piers along the Hudson River. The expanse of a pier seems to be a natural place for dogs to run, but again there is always the danger that your pooch will follow the frisbee or tennis ball he is chasing over the edge. Dogs also slip and fall into the water, or simply jump in for fun. Be careful, and again, keep the leashes on—owners have drowned trying to rescue their dogs.

Special Tours and Outings

Another wonderful option for exercising your pet is to take one of the many fascinating guided tours of New York City offered by **Sidewalks of New York,** 212-517-0210. This company conducts walking tours of various neighborhoods, or on specific themes. Well-behaved dogs are allowed to accompany you. Be sure to mention that you are bringing your dog when you make your reservation, and see that your dog minds his manners. On the tour, stay on the outskirts of the group, and be sensitive to other members who may be afraid of dogs. Sidewalks welcomes dogs on almost all tours except, of course, the "Tavern Tour,"

Maria Hansen and her Fidelco guide dog, Reno, pounding the pavement down the Great White Way. Maria is an actress and the New York chairperson and national co-chairperson for the Performers with Disabilities Committee of AFTRA (American Federation of TV and Radio Artists), which promotes acting opportunities for disabled individuals. Reno is Maria's constant companion, guiding her around New York to auditions and casting calls.

Credit: Fidelco Guide Dog Foundation

where health codes prevent him from "bellying up to the bar." Call them!

Liberty State Park—visible from the lower west side of Manhattan, across the Hudson in New Jersey—is accessible on weekends to city dogs via the **Hoboken–Battery Park Ferry,** 201-420-6307. This is the only ferry that accepts non-crated, leashed dogs (small dogs in crates are fine on the **Staten Island Ferry,** 718-390-5253, and larger dogs in crates are allowed by special reservation on the **Port Imperial Ferry,** 201-902-8850). The Hoboken–Battery Park Ferry docks behind the World Financial Center and takes you and your dog across the Hudson to the wonderful park, complete with stunning views of Manhattan, the Statue of Liberty, and New York harbor.

Blading, Biking, and Jogging with Your Dog

To give themselves *and* their dogs extra exercise, many New Yorkers choose to skate, bike, or jog with their dogs at their sides. When done safely, this can be a terrific exercise for both of you. This sort of exercise is only appropriate for mid-sized to large dogs who have long legs. It's just not fair to expect the little guys to keep up over long distances, no matter how quickly they can scamper about the apartment! Even with a big, enthusiastic dog, there are a few things to keep in mind.

You must condition your pet for strenuous exercise in the same way you would condition yourself: Start off slowly, then gradually increase the intensity of the workout. Check with your dog's veterinarian before you begin. Dogs suffer muscle aches, pains, and other exercise-related injuries just like their owners. If your dog has the potential for bone or muscle problems like hip dysplasia or arthritis, extended running could *really* make the problem worse. Young dogs under a year still have growing to do, and a lot of hard work could cause trouble down the road. Older, out-of-shape dogs have problems as well, and need time to become aerobically fit the same way people do.

While you can go and buy a new pair of running shoes when your old ones wear out, your dog is stuck with his pads. As tough as they look, a dog's paws may become worn and begin to bleed after as little as ten minutes of running on pavement. Again, start slowly. Foot pads will toughen up quickly if you give your dog three or four days' rest between your initial short runs.

Heat presents another problem. Don't run your dog on a hot day—in New York humidity, that means 85 degrees and above. The thickest paw pads are no match for New York summer pavement! Before you set off on your run, take the time to check the surface temperature of the road. If the asphalt is too hot for you to touch, don't risk your dog's paws. Dogs don't sweat as we do, and they cannot cool themselves down when they become overheated. If their body temperature goes up even 2 degrees from their normal temperature of 101 to 102 degrees, they can get heatstroke.

Don't make your dog a "weekend warrior" who gets dragged around the park a few times every Saturday when you get your bike out. He'll start off enthusiastically but will end up tenderfooted, tired, and possibly overheated, as well as stiff and sore for the next few days. Instead, introduce a regular exercise program slowly and carefully, the way you would for yourself. Never force a dog to run against his will, and if he seems reluctant, LEAVE HIM AT HOME!

Before you exercise, be sure you've replaced your dog's choke collar with a flat buckle collar, or better yet, a chest harness. He should be trained to "heel," meaning that he must run easily at your side, *not* weaving or crossing in front of you. Use a regular leather or nylon six- to eight-foot leash, not a flexi-leash, which can expand and pull you off balance when your dog suddenly veers off after a squirrel.

For safe bicycling with your dog, **Springer, Allenfarm,** 1627 Union Street, Bangor, ME 04401, 800-BIKE-K9S, has developed an aluminum arm that attaches to your leash from the bike's frame. It allows you to ride along without the fear of your dog crossing in front of you, thus causing a crash!

An older or smaller dog who can't run alongside your bicycle will be able to join you on your bike adventures if you fit your bike with a little trailer. **Cycle Tote,** Dept DF, North Link Lane, Ft. Collins, CO 80524, 800-747-2407, has designed a wonderful bike trailer in which your dog can ride safely, like a little pasha. Light and beautifully designed, this trailer also carries gear.

When roller-skating with your dog, you'll have to be much more aware of safety than you would be by yourself. *Always* be prepared to stop—FAST! Don't get going downhill so speedily that your dog can't keep up. You will probably have to "ride" the brake on the downhills, wearing it out more quickly, but don't get ahead of your dog! Practice braking when your dog is pulling hard. You might consider *adding a brake* to your other skate so that you'll be ready for anything. The more practiced and steady you are, the safer you'll both be.

Exercising your New York dog as you jog, bike, or skate can be a joy if you just approach it sensibly and ALWAYS CARRY WATER FOR YOUR DOG! Have fun!

Chapter 3

The Canine Gourmand and the Snappy Dresser in New York

Where to Get Food and Supplies for Your Canine Best Friend

Naturally, a city that offers you Hammacher Schlemmer, Barney's, and F.A.O. Schwarz, or Leo Lindy's and the Automat, is not to be outdone in the doggie realm. While the health department still frowns on your pooch accompanying you to dinner at The Rainbow Room (your dog can join you for al fresco dining at an outdoor cafe!), there is plenty of nourishment to be found in New York for your pet, and plenty of places to find the supplies and accoutrements to make your dog's life complete.

Any number of "bringing up baby" dog books will have all the advice you need for your dog. If I may suggest a book or two,

Recipe for Homemade Dog Biscuits

1 cup whole wheat flour
1 cup white flour
½ cup powdered milk
⅔ of a stick of margarine
1 egg
⅓ cup water
1 teaspoon brown sugar
1 jar baby food meat

Combine all ingredients. Mix and knead well. Roll out on a cookie sheet, and cut into bone shapes with a knife or cookie cutter. Bake at 325 degrees for thirty minutes. Allow to cool in oven.

Makes two dozen biscuits.

in my opinion you can't go wrong following the methods and approach to dog ownership described in either of the books by the monks of New Skete. *How to Be Your Dog's Best Friend: A Training Manual for Dog Owners* and *The Art of Raising a Puppy* have become indispensable sources of guidance and wisdom for many dog owners. Both are usually available at bookstores as well as pet supply shops.

The basic tools of dog ownership? Obviously you'll need a collar and leashes—a six-foot-long leather or nylon one, and a flexi- (expandable) leash. You'll need water and food bowls, although I'm sure your chipped Wedgwood will do in a pinch, and you'll probably want a crate. These are the barest of essentials, and the fact that Americans support a ten-billion-dollar-a-year pet supply industry suggests that you'll get a few more things as well.

Your Dog's Crate

In my opinion, a crate is a necessity. You probably think, "I would *never* put my dog in a cage," but properly used, a crate can be your dog's palace! Remember that dogs, like wolves, prefer to sleep in dens, small close spaces where they feel secure.

By providing your dog with a crate, you are giving him a private place all his own, where he can keep his toys and his blanket and where he can go to chill out. Besides, if you're ever going to travel with your dog, you will need a crate. If he ever spends time at the groomer's or the veterinarian's, he will be put in a crate. So, if you use one at home, and he is accustomed to it, those visits will go more smoothly.

A crate should come as standard equipment with a new puppy, because using one makes house-breaking a breeze! Usually, dogs won't soil where they sleep, so if you routinely put your puppy in his crate when you're not supervising him, he won't have an "accident." Simply *whisk* him straight outside when you let him out of his crate, and he'll easily learn that *outside* is where business is done. Obviously, I'm not suggesting that you confine a puppy or any dog to a crate all the time except when they need to go out. It should simply be used as a helpful aid. If your puppy is snoozing, or chewing on his favorite toy in his crate while you're out running errands, he's *not* shredding the couch, teething on your Louis XIV chair, or making a mess on the oriental. Yes, there will be accidents, but using a crate makes house-breaking 80 percent easier.

If you have an older dog who, despite your best training efforts, continues to do destructive things in your absence, you should consider using a crate. It's simpler, pleasanter, easier on your blood pressure (and your pocketbook), and kinder to your dog!

So where to go to get that crate? Where should you get your dog's food? Pet stores, veterinarians' offices, and dog-grooming shops now sell dog food and, frequently, a few other supplies. It is also useful to know that many stores will deliver to your home, which, in the case of a fifty-pound bag of dog food or a crate, can be a blessing! There's a whole world of canine catalogues from which you can buy things through mail order, sometimes at a pretty big discount.

To get you started, here are a few of the most remarkable *not-to-be-missed* stores that sell food and supplies to the New York dog:

MANHATTAN

Uptown

Fuzzy Muzzles, 4915 Broadway (near 207th Street), 212-567-4773

An adorable shop with a wonderful "dog bar" outside for thirsty canines. All supplies and foods are available, as well as grooming. A great addition to the neighborhood.

Creature Comforts, 2778 Broadway (at 107th Street), 212-864-9964

A big, friendly shop with all the necessities. Grooming and free delivery are available.

West Side

The Pet Stop, 554 Columbus Avenue (between 86th and 87th streets), 212-580-2400

Over 400 different kinds of dog foods and tons of supplies, especially natural food and "natural alternatives." Helpful staff. Free delivery.

The Pet Bowl, 440 Amsterdam Avenue (the corner of 81st Street), 212-595-4200

Full of foods and accessories. Free delivery. Treats for your dog while you browse!

The Pet Market, 210 West 72nd Street (west of Broadway), 212-799-4200

Discount dog foods and supplies; added discounts on bulk orders. Specialized diets and "hypoallergenic foods."

The Pet Department Store, 233 West 54th Street (between 8th and 9th avenues), 212-489-9195

One of midtown's most necessary shopping stops. Offers a huge selection of food and supplies, plus an amazing assortment of doggie clothes by such designers as Ruff Lauren, Mary McFido, and Calvin Canine. A "spa day of beauty," including massage, is available for your dog at their grooming salon.

East Side

Karen's for People & Pets, 1195 Lexington Avenue (at 81st Street), 212-472-9440

The way Holly Golightly went to Tiffany's, my friends go to Karen's when they get a case of the "mean reds." Designer/owner Karen features unique, custom pet togs and accessories, with matching ensembles for owners. They carry a full array of treats and toys, as well as books. Food, other supplies, and grooming are also available.

Trolek Moves to New York

Sometimes the greatest challenge to getting your dog fed is finding out what he or she will eat. One day in the park I got into a conversation with a man walking a German shepherd named Trolek. He told me that Trolek really belonged to his aged grandmother in Warsaw. Two summers earlier the grandmother and Trolek had spent a month in New York. Recently she had become too frail to care for the dog, and rather than give Trolek away to a neighbor in Poland, she had put him on a plane to New York.

Trolek had arrived safely, but was not eating well. No matter what brand of food the grandson offered him, Trolek sniffed it with disdain and refused to eat it. After a week, the grandson was distraught. He knew the old dog was not strong enough to withstand the fast for very long.

Desperately, the grandson had experimented with different kinds of dog food, from supermarket brands to expensive "designer" foods. He even got down on the floor and pantomimed eating the food himself. Every time, Trolek sniffed the food, regarded the grandson disappointedly, and walked away.

I looked at Trolek. He did walk a little stiffly, but that's practically normal for an old shepherd. He didn't seem too depressed as he nosed about with Serena. But under his plush coat, his ribs were showing. I wondered how he had behaved the summer he had visited New York with the grandmother. "What did he eat then?" I asked.

"Well, that was different; my grandmother cooked for him," the grandson replied.

"What do you mean?"

"She loves to cook. Every day she cooked dinner for me and Trolek. On nights I ate out, she cooked for him."

"Cooked what?"

"Stews, chicken pies, marrow bones, some Polish stuff too, you know, sausages, pierogi."

"Did she cook for him at home in Poland?"

"I guess," he admitted. "She's always in the kitchen, and after my grandfather died, there was just Trolek."

"You're surprised that this dog won't eat dog food?" I asked incredulously.

Here was a dog who had probably spent every afternoon in the kitchen at his mistress's feet while she cooked. Preparing to eat had been a production, surrounded by wonderful smells, the warmth of the stove, and the company of his beloved mistress. I imagined that old Trolek associated food with much more than simply filling his stomach. No wonder dinnertime in his new life seemed drab and unappetizing.

"Oh no," said the man, guessing my thoughts, "I am not cooking for this dog!"

"Well, why don't you try pretending to cook then?" I asked. "Don't just plop the dog food out of the can into his dish, make a production of it, fuss over it, heat it up, mix in whatever is left from your dinner."

We met again a week or so later. Trolek looked great. "It worked!" said the man. "I mixed in my dinner, some leftover oatmeal, even a carton of old Chinese food, and he ate like a champ. Then I snuck some dog food in, and now he's eating that too."

"That's great," I said.

"Now," he replied, "if I could only get him not to sleep in bed with me."

Peter's Emporium for Pets, 1449 Second Avenue (at 76th Street), 212-772-3647

"The Gap for Dogs," a wonderful resource. Food, clothes, et al. The hand-painted ceramic dog bowls are a must have. They'll put your Italian pottery to shame.

Pet Necessities, 236 East 75th Street (between 2nd and 3rd avenues), 212-988-0769

Next to the Center for Veterinary Care, this well-stocked shop has every kind of accessory and pet-care product you might need. Delivery is available.

Animal Attractions, 335 East 65th Street (between 1st and 2nd avenues), 212-734-8400

A full line of dog foods and accessories, knowledgeable staff, natural and herbal products. Free delivery.

Sutton Dog Parlor, 311 East 60th Street (between 1st and 2nd avenues), 212-355-2850

Home of the Doggie Deli. Treat your pup to a "pet pizza" or a "doggie pop." Carnegie Deli, watch out!

Pampered Paws, 227 East 57th Street (between 2nd and 3rd avenues), 212-935-PAWS

"New York's most exclusive dog and cat boutique."

Everything your canine's heart desires. Weekday free delivery in Manhattan and to Roosevelt Island.

Midtown

Animal Crackers, 159 East 33rd Street (between Lexington and 3rd avenues), 212-725-1970
Food, supplies, treats, and crates. Free delivery.

Doggie-Do & Pussycats, Too, 230 East 29th Street (between 2nd and 3rd avenues), 212-679-7888
The place for canine couture! A wide selection of "doggie clothes," from conservative pin-striped coats to leather biker jackets. Collars and leashes from elegant leather to rhinestone glitz! Food, supplies, and grooming are also available.

Animal World, 219 East 26th Street (between 2nd and 3rd avenues), 212-685-0027
Accessories and lots of food, especially hard-to-find brands (even Abady, the impossible-to-find food I feed Serena); they will deliver and ship anywhere.

Chelsea

The Barking Zoo, 172 Ninth Avenue (between 20th and 21st streets), 212-255-0658
This well-stocked shop also serves as a neighborhood/city info center to canine happenings in the Big Apple. When you stop in, be sure to pet the resident greyhounds, get a copy of their most recent newsletter/flyer, and put your dog's picture up on their "Wall of Fame."

Downtown

Whiskers, The Natural Pet Supply Co., 235 East 9th Street, 212-979-2532
Holistic/organic foods as well as homeopathic and herbal treatments for your pets. A marvelous, magical store—see the section on extra-special catalogues for more about Whiskers.

Beasty Feast, 237 Bleecker Street (between Carmine and Leroy streets), 212-243-3261; 630 Hudson Street (at Jane Street), 212-620-7099
Two downtown locations. Discounts on all brands of dog food and pet accessories.

"No, my name is not Beethoven!" Ramphis is a Saint Bernard owned by caterer Penny Miller. Penny says she is tempted to hang a tape recorder around Ramphis's neck that plays "My name is not Beethoven, it is Ramphis. I weigh one hundred and eighty-five pounds. I eat two or three cups of food, twice a day. I only take up as much space in the apartment as I need to lie down in. The city is not too small for me. I am very happy living here." This way, Penny could simply push the "Play" button on the recorder and not spend every walk with Ramphis answering questions from curious people on the street. Here, Ramphis baby-sits in Central Park. Credit: Petography

Dee's Doggie & Cat Diner, 176 West Houston Street (at 6th Avenue), 212-989-4407

Great line of foods and accessories at the lowest prices possible. A great neighborhood resource, they are very helpful in recommending area veterinarians and dog walkers.

Dudley's Paw, 327 Greenwich Street, 212-966-5167

Meet the ubiquitous Dudley (a mixed-breed sweetie) and browse through the wide selection of foods, supplies, and treats. The handmade-to-order dog sweaters, and the imported collars, are especially wonderful.

Little Arf'n Annie, 458 Broome Street, 212-431-1682

Lots of food, some supplies. So downtown "SoHo cool" that you expect to see dogs wearing shades and Doc Martens exiting the store.

Le Pet Spa, 300 Rector Place (in Battery Park City), 212-786-9070

Battery Park City proves once again that it could exist as a sovereign state. Full line of dog foods and supplies. Grooming and veterinarian services are also offered.

BROOKLYN

Brooklyn Heights

Beastly Bites, 140 Court Street (between Atlantic Avenue and Pacific Street), 718-522-5133

All the accessories your dog might need, as well as the best foods at discounted prices.

Peter's Emporium, 105 Montague Street (between Hicks and Henry streets), 718-624-2533

Many brands of dog food and necessary supplies.

Bay Ridge

Animal Pantry, 697 86th Street (and 7th Avenue), 718-680-2220

Bowls, brushes, leashes. Food and more. Delivery is available.

from "The Dog That Bit People"

. . . Muggs at his meals was an unusual sight. Because of the fact that if you reached towards the floor he would bite you, we usually put his food plate on top of an old kitchen table with a bench alongside the table. Muggs would stand on the bench and eat. I remember that my mother's Uncle Horatio, who boasted that he was the third man up Missionary Ridge, was sputteringly indignant when he found out that we fed the dog on a table because we were afraid to put his food on the floor. He said he wasn't afraid of any dog that ever lived and that he would put the dog's plate on the floor if we would give it to him. Robert said that if Uncle Horatio had fed Muggs on the ground just before the battle he would have been the first man up Missionary Ridge. Uncle Horatio was furious. "Bring him in! Bring him in now!" he shouted. "I'll feed the —— on the floor!" Robert was all for giving him a chance, but my father wouldn't hear of it. He said that Muggs had already been fed. "I'll feed him again," bawled Uncle Horatio. We had quite a time quieting him.

—*James Thurber*

Park Slope

Mother's Pet Food & Accessories, 370 7th Avenue (corner of 11th Street), 718-788-8688

One of my favorite shops. The very best in foods and supplies (even Abady!). Knowledgeable, helpful staff. An important neighborhood resource offering referrals for veterinarians, dog walkers, and pet-sitters, as well as free training advice from brilliant trainer Terry Firth one Saturday a month.

Sheepshead Bay

Groomingdales Pet Salon & Boutique, 2319 Voorhees Avenue, 718-934-6756

Bloomies for dogs! They carry over 1,000 different coats, sweaters, hats, and rainwear for the well-tailored pooch. Grooming and supplies are available as well.

THE BRONX

Animal Feeds Inc., 3255 Park Avenue (corner of 163rd Street), 718-293-7750
Food, supplies, accessories, and clothes for your pet.

Pets Are Fun, 5626A Mosholu Avenue (at 259th Street), 718-601-6585
All sorts of supplies, accessories, and food.

QUEENS

Pet Menu, 215-05 Northern Boulevard (two blocks east of Bell Boulevard), Bayside, 718-224-4PET
All the best foods. Accessories, supplies, and toys; delivery is available.

K-9 Caterers, 82-02 Cooper Avenue, Glendale, 718-275-5614; 89-50 Metropolitan Avenue, Rego Park
"The pet nutrition pro shop." Wholesale prices for almost every brand of dog food. Supplies and accessories as well.

The Pet Nosh, 245-07 Northern Boulevard, Little Neck, 718-229-8976
Discount foods and supplies with special diets available; also clothing and accessories.

Catalogue Shopping

It's no surprise that there is a world of catalogue shopping available to your dog. The real question is: Why not a Doggie Home Shopping Network? New Yorkers are surrounded by pet supply merchants, so we enjoy an incredible diversity of items. But sometimes it does pay to order through catalogues, since they frequently offer their merchandise at discounted or wholesale prices. This can make a difference financially, especially if you need a big-ticket item like an airline crate for a Saint Bernard. All the catalogues feature an array of "basics": leashes, collars, shampoos, flea and tick collars and treatments, dog toys and treats, airline crates and cages, dog beds, mats, and books on dogs. Some specialize in particular items, but they are all good resources for the dog owner.

Here is a listing of some of the better-known catalogues of dog products:

R.C. Steele, 1989 Transit Way, Box 910, Brock-port, NY 14420, 800-872-3773
A giant wholesaler, they require a $50 minimum purchase.

J-B Pet Supplies, 289 Wagaraw Road, Hawthorne, NJ 07506, 201-432-2222
Everything you'll need for your dog. Especially wonderful book selection.

Pedigrees, Box 905, DF 1760, Brockport, NY 14420, 800-437-8434
"The catalogue for pets and their people." Good stuff, loads of clothes, and lots of FUN! Always features a stylish "Cover Dog."

Care-a-Lot, 1617 Diamond Springs Road, Virginia Beach, VA 23455, 804-460-9771
Specializes in show training and professional grooming supplies in addition to the basics.

Doctors Foster & Smith, P.O. Box 100, Rhinelander, WI 54501, 800-334-3699
"Pet supply and health care catalogue." Basics, plus every kind of vaccine and medicine you can imagine. An education just to read. Equals one semester at Cornell Veterinary School.

Upco-Dept. 10, P.O. Box 969, St. Joseph, MO 64502, 816-233-8800
"Over forty years in the business." Industry leader offering high-quality, innovative, and practical pet care items.

The Mail Order Pet Shop, 250W Executive Drive, Englewood, NJ 11717, 800-366-7387
Especially helpful on the phone. "8,500 products for your pets."

Natural Animal, Department D, P.O. Box 1177, St. Augustine, FL 32085, 800-274-7387
  Environmentally safe products. Mostly shampoos and dips. If you do your laundry at "Eco Wash," this catalogue is for you.

J-B Wholesale, 5 Raritan Road, Oakland, NJ 07436, 800-526-0388
  The motherlode of pet supplies. Minimum order $25. Offers a super-sweepstakes entry with every order. The winter '94 sweepstakes prize was a trip to London— to attend Crufts, the grandest dog show in England, the equivalent of our Westminster.

Extra-Special Catalogues

Whiskers Health Food & Products for Pets, 235 East 9th Street, New York, NY 10003, 800-WHISKERS (944-7537), is a marvelous pet supply store in the Village that also puts out a terrific catalogue. Whiskers represents "the new world of alternatives in pet health care and lifestyle," meaning that they embrace and offer an introduction to living as naturally as possible with your animal. All the products they carry are all-natural, free of chemicals and preservatives. The shampoos and dips are the safest, the foods the most wholesome, and the books and tapes they carry full of information about "natural living." They carry a complete line of homeopathic treatments, herbal and flower remedies, vitamins and supplements. Membership in Whiskers' "health club" allows you to try new products at a 10 percent discount. Other club benefits include a bimonthly newsletter, a free subscription to *The Natural Pet* magazine, product/seminar information, and further discounts. If you shop in health food stores for yourself and your family, Whiskers is where you should be getting your pet supplies.

  Dog Goods Ltd., 2035 West Wabansia, Chicago, IL 60647, 800-736-4746, is the brainchild of champion equestrienne and lifelong dog lover Carolyn Lackey, who began fashioning collars for her dogs out of the extra parts of the beautiful English leather bridles her show jumpers wore. Her classic collection includes the best accoutrements for dogs, from the original collars and leads to adorable and *practical* cotton "panties" in several gingham patterns that hide the pads you *must* use for your female when she is in season. For sight hounds, she offers classic "wide" collars that are safer and also accentuate the beautiful line of a noble neck and head, reminiscent of a more romantic time.

In the Company of Dogs, 800-964-3647. Picture a Spiegel catalogue for canines. Here, dog products are presented in a "lifestyle setting." Fabulous, exclusively designed collars, leashes, bowls, and jewelry (for you) join stylish dog beds, pet ottomans in home decor fabrics, accessories, and holiday gifts—which can often be personalized. It is simply a knockout catalogue, with a sophisticated, glamorous style—for both dogs and their owners.

Blue Ribbons Pet Products, 75 Modular Avenue, Commack, NY 11725, 516-864-1555, is a charming catalogue of doggie things, with an emphasis on natural products.

A Bide-A-Wee Story

During the devastating floods that racked the Midwest during the summer of 1993, thousands lost their homes and possessions. Animals as well as humans were caught in the deadly path of the floods. The following autumn, New York talk show host Sally Jesse Raphael had a show highlighting some of the tragic personal stories from the flood. In each case, the producers of her show attempted to compensate the victims in some way for their loss.

Among the flood victims covered on Sally's show was a young boy from Missouri, whose family had lost their house in the floods and whose dog had drowned. The family had been away helping other victims, and when they arrived home, their own home with their dog in it had been consumed by the waters.

In anticipation of this heartrending tale, the producers of Sally's show had arranged in advance with the boy's parents to get him another dog. The Bide-A-Wee Home Association Shelter, on East 38th Street, was brought in on the plan. A few months earlier a pregnant golden retriever had been abandoned and was accepted into Bide-A-Wee's shelter. She had produced a beautiful litter of puppies, which were just old enough to be adopted.

The family was flown to New York for the taping. There was barely a dry eye in the studio as the young boy told of finding his dog drowned. After a pause, an attendant from Bide-A-Wee brought out one of the adorable pups. The look of ecstasy that crossed the boy's face as he took his new pup in his arms sent all watching reaching for the Kleenex once again. A boy who had lost his own pet paired with a pup abandoned before birth. It was television perfect.

Chapter 4

"Style Me, Baby!"

Groomers Who Beautify the New York Dog

S o your cosmopolitan canine has eaten a wonderful meal and is on the way home from her first walk. Everything is going perfectly. As you are about to cross the avenue, a city bus drives through one of those sinister puddles by the curb. A tsunami drenches your startled pooch.

You manage to get her up to your apartment, closing her in the kitchen. The phone rings, and as you talk, you can hear your dog shaking herself dry all over your cabinets. This dog needs scrubbing, and the mere thought of the job exhausts you. You can't do it, but somebody has to. Where do you turn?

Aside from the everyday disasters like the one I just described, all dogs need some grooming. Even breeds that don't require "styling" must have their toenails, matted hair, and dirty ears attended to.

It is not difficult to help your dog with his personal hygiene. A weekly (daily during shedding time) brushing makes the difference between a kempt and an unkempt pet. It also leaves your dog feeling loved and cared for. Be sure to brush sensitive areas gently: Never bear down too hard. If your vet shows you how, you can keep on top of toenails and dirty ears as well and, if you don't mind, baths and flea dips can be done in your tub.

Of course you might not want to deal with hefting that 120-pound Akita into your bathtub. This is why we have been blessed with professional dog groomers. The hair artisans of the dog world, they magically turn our dirty, smelly canine companions back into huggable bundles of love.

Many breeds need professional help to remain recognizable (the untutored eye *might* mistake an unclipped white poodle for a bichon frise!). To make your life easier, and to keep the "bad hair day" breeds looking spiffy, there are groomers all over New York City who offer basic services and specialized treatments. It is the groomer's job to know the various clips and cuts appropriate for each breed of dog. However, if you are planning to show your dog, and own a breed which must be groomed to a very particular "standard" set by the American or United Kennel Club, you might want to find a groomer who specializes in your breed.

Grooming for shows is a complex and exacting business. Various terrier breeds, for instance, must have their coats "hand stripped" to be admissible in the showring. A time-intensive process which involves removing the dead hair in the undercoat and thinning the entire coat evenly with a stripping knife, hand-stripping is considered among the highest forms of artistry in the world of dog grooming. When done correctly, the process is entirely painless for the dog, since only dead hair is pulled out, and the texture and rich color of the coarser outer coat is maintained, leaving a beautiful finish and sheen.

Many breeds do not shed. Their hair simply grows, and must be tended to as you would your own. Of course this means no shedding, and much less dander in the fur—the bane of the allergic person—but it also means more upkeep. Soft-coated dogs such as bichons and Maltese need to be hand scissored to get the best effect on their particular coats, while most other breeds can be clipped with electric clippers, or clipped and scissored, to achieve a showring appearance.

I was once at Westminster watching the standard poodles near the ring gate where the dogs go in and out. A competitor was waiting for the next class, holding a gorgeous, sparkling-white poodle bitch. Around her head and neck, her coat had been teased and her hair sprayed into a huge alabaster mane, her nails lacquered, her batting eyelashes curled. She was the ultimate in canine glamour and sex appeal. In the ring, an equally stunning black poodle diva was mesmerizing the crowd with her coif and attitude. She was working that ring (picture Ru Paul as a dog). The white poodle's handler was the partner of the black dog's exhibitor. "I'm telling you," he gushed to a friend, "with these two at home, it's like living with Marilyn Monroe and Diana Ross!"

If you are not going to show your dog, there is no reason to go to all the expense of hand-stripping or intricate clips. There are serviceable, attractive, less elaborate cuts and procedures that won't take such a bite out of your wallet but will still leave your dog well groomed and comfortable. A reputable groomer will work with you in this regard. Beware of those who snobbishly tell you that a clip or treatment "must" be done one way or another.

All dogs benefit from a trip to the groomer. Properly done, a grooming is a health benefit as well as an aesthetic treatment. In addition to bathing and styling the coat, groomers will trim the hair between the pads on his paws, which can knot, causing a stone-in-shoe effect to the dog; they will also clean the ears, genitals, and around the anus with a medicated solution and will safely trim the toenails.

Groomers offer many special treatments, from hot oil and sulphur baths for dogs with skin problems to antistatic treatments for their hair. Even antiallergy washes can be applied to your dog's coat. These decrease the amount of dander he gives off, helping the allergic dog lovers in your home. Obviously fleas and ticks are a concern, and your groomer can help you combat that yearly onslaught with effective, less toxic products than those you might commonly buy.

Teeth Cleaning and Anal Glands

Some groomers include cleaning your dog's teeth, but this procedure is best left to your veterinarian. A complete teeth cleaning must be done with the dog anesthetized—not the undertaking of a groomer! Simply running their finger covered in gauze over the dog's teeth and scraping the plaque with a fingernail does not substitute for a thorough cleaning. Your veterinarian can give your dog's teeth a thorough cleaning when needed, and *you* should do the daily brushing.

Yes, as silly as it sounds, you should brush your dog's teeth

(Don't!) Give That Dog a Bone

Dogs love to gnaw on bones. Few things please them so much as sneaking off to a favorite corner with a lovely section of cow femur full of marrow to work on. However, the only really safe bones to give to dogs are well-boiled beef knuckles or a part of the long leg bone, also boiled. NEVER give your dog any kind of poultry, lamb, pork, or veal bones. These break into brittle shards and can cause serious damage. For your dog's safety, you must be vigilant. Even the best-behaved dog is liable to plunder the garbage when tempted, so protect them from themselves! Offer safe rawhide (see chapter five, page 80) or nylon pseudobones as a substitute. Your dog will still try to convince you that it would really be okay to slip him that chicken leg, but don't believe it!

every day at home. Their teeth are subject to periodontal disease and decay in the same way as ours. But don't read this and grab the tube of Crest. You'll need doggie toothpaste—which doesn't foam and is flavored with the tastes dogs *want* in their mouths, like chicken or liver. In most pet stores you can buy a kit containing paste, a toothbrush, and a few "dental wipes," breath-freshening tissues to rub over your dog's teeth.

Unless you've been brushing your canine's canines since his puppyhood, this is going to come as a rude surprise to him. Go slowly. Start by rubbing your finger over his teeth and gums and move up to a finger with a little paste on it. If all goes well, next time you can introduce the brush. Serena never progressed to the brush. She hated it, so I got her a little "finger brush." This is sort of an extended plastic thimble with bristles, which works pretty well.

You can also buy dog toys that help clean teeth and freshen breath. **Dental Kong**, available in most pet supply stores, is a dog toy which reduces plaque and helps reduce bad breath. **Nylabone** offers several dog toy products which reduce plaque as your dog plays with them: Nylafloss, a knot of ham-bone-flavored nylon, which works the same way your dental floss does, and Plaque Attacker, which has raised "dental tips" to get between teeth as your dog chews.

Some groomers also offer to expel your dog's anal glands, again, something best left to your vet. These glands are small "sacks" on either side of the rectum which inflate and deflate in the course of your dog's evacuation. When impacted, the glands don't deflate properly during the normal course of business and become uncomfortable. Dogs will try to alleviate the discomfort themselves by dragging their backsides along the ground. Only a veterinarian or trained vet tech should attempt to expel the glands. Obviously it is a delicate business, and if it's done incorrectly it can cause serious damage—an abscess or rupture of the glands.

Using Tranquilizers

Many people have the misconception that groomers tranquilize or otherwise sedate dogs in order to work on them. This is not, and should not, be the case. Nobody but a vet or vet tech should "tranq" a dog. I think the myth about groomers grew because dog owners cannot imagine their squirmy, sometimes hyperactive pets holding still for long enough to be trimmed with scissors or clippers without "chemical" persuasion. What people underestimate is both the professionalism of a good groomer and their dog's ability to rise to an occasion and behave himself.

A good groomer is an experienced dog handler, relating to a client's dog in much the same way as a professional dog trainer would. Have you ever noticed that the problem dog in a training class, completely out of control in the hands of his owner, becomes the model pupil when the trainer takes the leash? Dogs innately respect authority and professionalism—traits a good groomer will have and which the dog's owner may lack.

If a responsible groomer encounters a dog who simply will not allow himself to be handled, they will not persist but will call the owner and make other arrangements. Perhaps the dog's veterinarian will be consulted to prescribe a sedative, or the owner will have to practice body handling to accustom the dog to being worked on before another appointment is made.

Finding a Groomer

The best thing an owner can do to ensure a dog's happy future at the grooming salon is to start early. The sooner a dog is exposed to handling, the easier the process will be. Puppies can safely go to the grooming shop for a bath, ear cleaning, and nail clipping as soon as they complete their series of shots (usually at three months).

When looking for a reputable groomer, there are several important things to keep in mind. A clean, well-run shop looks it. As you know from the barber's or the hairdresser's, hair on the floor doesn't necessarily mean the establishment is not kept up. During a busy grooming day there will be hair on the floor of the most professional shop.

Things which should press your warning button are an unpleasant smell or the refusal to let you see the back area where the dogs are groomed. This does not mean that you should disrupt business by touring the room with a white glove, but a reputable place with nothing to hide should let you take a quick peek into the grooming area.

If you are a nonsmoker, make sure that the shop you send your dog to does not permit smoking on the premises; otherwise your expensively cleaned dog may come home smelling of cigarette smoke. Dogs are regularly kept in crates or wire cages while waiting their turns in the bathtub, on the grooming table, and when they are waiting to go home. If you see any fecal matter or urine in a cage with a dog—lazy groomers may let a dog sit in a mess until it is his turn to be groomed—that would be a reason to not use the shop. In general, use your New York savvy! If the shop makes you feel the least bit uncomfortable, go elsewhere.

Dog groomers do not need to be licensed, as hairdressers do. They don't even need any formal training. In fact, it is possible for an excellent groomer to have learned the craft by apprenticing to a knowledgeable professional.

There are courses and academies that offer degrees in dog grooming. Graduation from such an institution is verification that the particular groomer knows his/her craft. Membership in the National Dog Groomers Association, which provides certification programs and continuing education workshops to keep members updated on current trends and advances in the industry, is another measure of competency.

Sometimes the best groomers have neither a degree nor membership in a professional association. They are simply dog-

"I Think My Dog Is in Heat: What Should I Do?"

Have little red drops suddenly appeared on the kitchen linoleum? Does your female dog attend to her personal hygiene more studiously than usual? Has she become the most popular girl in the dog group? If you are not sure she is spayed, it is possible that your dog has gone into "heat," or estrus.

Female dogs pass through estrus twice a year, beginning at around six to ten months and continuing through life at roughly six-month intervals. To make things simple, let's call the day you first notice blood day one.

During these first six to twelve days of "proestrus," the shedding of the old uterine lining, her discharge will go from pure blood to an almost clear fluid. To protect your rugs from the spots, you can buy one of those little doggie sanitary pad ensembles.

When the fluid has changed color, you can be pretty sure that she is in estrus, the fertile period of the cycle. Estrus lasts another nine to twelve days, actual ovulation usually taking place within the first forty-eight hours. Basically: YOUR DOG HAS BECOME A TICKING PUPPY BOMB! ONLY LET HER OUT OF THE HOUSE WITH EXTREME CAUTION! SHE IS FERTILE! SHE WILL BREED!

Don't trust her, and don't believe a word she says. She will do extraordinary things to meet a boyfriend—females dogs closed in crates have been known to push back against the wire, enabling a male outside the crate to breed with them! What then to do if your dog is in heat? Lock her in the highest, most remote bell tower of St. Patrick's Cathedral for a month. Seriously, only let her out of the apartment under the closest supervision. This is definitely one of those situations where an ounce of prevention is worth a pound of cure.

When you add the six to twelve days of proestrus, with the nine to twelve days of estrus, the whole business will take the better part of a month. You can relax when you know a full month has passed.

If through some horrible mistake a male gets to your girl and they begin to do what comes naturally, the jig is up. If he has penetrated her, don't try to pull the lovers apart—it can seriously injure both dogs. Sit down and plan a visit to your vet. Protect your dog. Please don't let a mismating during your dog's heat cycle lead to an unwanted pregnancy.

friendly Edward Scissorhands. Follow your instincts and find a good shop. There are plenty of groomers in New York to choose from. As always, recommendations from a veterinarian or friend can help you find one to suit your dog's needs.

To get you started, here are some of the better-known New York dog grooming shops:

MANHATTAN

West Side

Fuzzy Muzzles, 4915 Broadway (near 207th Street), 212-567-4773
Features a "dog bar" outside for thirsty canine passersby.

Amsterdog Groomers, 586 Amsterdam Avenue (between 88th and 89th streets), 212-496-6117
Good reputation, nice people.

A Cut Above, 207 West 75th Street (between Broadway and Amsterdam), 212-799-TRIM
Features pickup and delivery service, which is very convenient, as well as hot oil treatments, organic dips, and hand-scissoring.

The Pet Department Store, 233 West 54th Street (between Broadway and 8th Avenue), 212-489-9195
Practically a Georgette Klinger Salon for dogs. All the usual services plus antistress, injury-specific, and postsurgical massage for your dog.

East Side

Groom and Tailor by Revi, 506 East 82nd Street (at York Avenue), 212-439-0679
Specializes in bichons!

Karen's for People & Pets, 1195 Lexington Avenue (81st Street), 212-472-9440
They do a beautiful job.

Le Chien Pet Salon, 1461A First Avenue (between 76th and 77th streets), 212-861-8100
Super, professional staff with many years of experience.

Canine Styles, 830 Lexington Avenue (between 63rd and 64th streets), 212-751-4549

The classic! New York's chicest salon, where the very poshest pooches let their hair down and are primped for their luncheon dates at Le Cirque.

New York School of Dog Grooming, 248 East 34th Street (off 2nd Avenue), 212-685-3776

Where it all begins! The only professional grooming school in NYC, it offers complete services as well.

Doggie-Do & Pussycats, Too, 230 East 29th Street (between 2nd and 3rd avenues), 212-679-7888

Home of my very favorite groomer, Larry Roth, who works magic with dog hair.

Downtown

Dog-O-Rama, 1617 Seventh Avenue South (between 10th and 11th streets), 212-627-3647

Specializing in creative cutting and coloring for "downtown punk pooches."

Le Pet Spa, 300 Rector Place (in Battery Park City), 212-786-9070

A great resource for Battery Park City pets.

Another "quintessentially New York" option is the magical **Laundermutt,** 45 Grove Street (off Bleecker Street), 212-691-7700. Conceived of and run by Beverly Hill, Laundermutt is a full-service grooming shop—*where you do the grooming*! Rather than paying grooming salon prices, or dealing with the unavoidable mess of washing your dog in your apartment, Laundermutt supplies you with everything you need to bathe and dry your dog on their premises. You just do the work, like a laundromat where you bring your dirty clothes. Call ahead for an appointment, and Laundermutt will supply the shampoo, conditioners, professional dryers, and lots of cookies. Prices range from $10 to $35 depending on the size of the dog. They also stock a wide selection of pet supplies and foods.

BROOKLYN

A Tailored Pet, 89 Pineapple Street, Brooklyn Heights, 718-875-7387

A very busy shop with reasonable prices. Call a few days ahead for an appointment.

Ronnie's, 346 39th Street (between 3rd and 4th avenues), 718-499-2021
Pickup and delivery, serving all of Brooklyn.

QUEENS

Queens has several groomers who have "scissors to go." They've equipped themselves with vans featuring hot and cold running water, dryers, and tables, and they've taken to the road. You can call any of these to arrange an appointment and they will pull up outside your building and groom your dog. Pretty neat, huh?

The Petmobile, 800-RUB-A-DUB (782-2382)
Best Mobile Dog Grooming, 718-347-6557
The Mobile Clipper, 718-417-3051

THE BRONX

Dog Charm Studio, 69 Harney Road (Exit 10, Bronx River Parkway), 914-725-5665
This shop serves the Bronx from Scarsdale. You'll need a car, but they're very good.

Riverdale Dog Grooming, 432 West 238th Street, 718-884-7575
All services are available at this friendly shop.

The Discount Dog Laundry

Something really wonderful is going on uptown in Manhattan. The Animal Rescue Network of East Harlem, a not-for-profit group working within the community to help abandoned and homeless animals, has opened **The Discount Dog Laundry, 212-860-7746**, a great program to raise badly needed funds, *and* assist pet owners in the area.

Because of the many wild or feral dogs and cats in East Harlem, diseases like rabies, distemper, and parvovirus, unheard of downtown, still exist. Low-income pet owners don't always have the money for basic veterinary care. Some can't even afford to immunize their pets.

In an effort to address these problems, the Rescue Network,

The Discount Dog Laundry is in full swing! While Robert and Rodney Smith attend to a white German shepherd, Feliciana Ortiz helps bathe a Viszla, and her sister, Euginie, grooms a mixed breed. The volunteers are paid in credit vouchers that are good for services at a local veterinarian. All the dogs in the photo were rescued from New York streets by the Animal Rescue Network of East Harlem and placed in permanent homes. Credit: Irene Smith and the East Harlem Veterinary Clinic, worked together to create the Discount Dog Laundry. If you live on Manhattan's east side, above 79th Street, volunteers from the Rescue Network will pick up your dog, take him to the "salon," and get him cleaned up. They offer basic bathing, flea-dipping, and brushing. When he's all dry and beautiful, they'll deliver him home to you. You pay only $20 to $30 depending on the size of your dog.

The volunteers who work at the Discount Dog Laundry earn vouchers for free veterinary care at the East Harlem Veterinary Clinic. The hard work they do gets their *own* pets necessary medical care.

The Animal Rescue Network of East Harlem's Discount Dog Laundry is a fantastic service, and a perfect example of a community working together to make things better.

Chapter 5

Someone to Watch Over ... Your Dog

Dog Walkers, Pet-Sitters, and Boarding Options

At some point in your dog-owning career, you won't be able to get home in time to take care of your pet. You'll work late, you'll need to go out of the city for a few days, or you'll plan a vacation. After you've exhausted imposing on friends or relatives, you'll need to seek professional help.

Your dog has *lots* of options in your absence. He can be cared for by a professional pet-sitter or dog walker, who will cater to his needs in your home. He can while away the hours merrily playing with pals at a doggie day care center. He can pack a little bag and go off to a dog bed and breakfast with posh accommodations. Or he can spend the time in the country at a traditional boarding kennel. As usual, your New York City dog's options are practically as interesting and varied as your own!

Let's take a closer look at some of the choices.

Dog Walkers

Even when you *are* in town, getting home in time to walk your dog regularly can be difficult. An emergency at work, a conference with your child's teacher, any number of things can prevent you from walking across the threshold exactly ten hours from the time you left. (Most healthy, mature dogs are capable of waiting ten hours while their owners are at work—puppies and older dogs with problems *must not* be expected to wait so long.)

And so, we have been blessed with dog walkers. A caring, dog-friendly professional who stops by your house and takes your dog on a long walk, providing "airing," exercise, and a certain amount of socialization and training. You return home, and your previously frantic-to-get-to-the-curb dog has already been out. He's relaxed, happy to see you, just pouring himself a highball.

Sounds great? Dog walkers are the greatest thing since the dishwasher! But, of course, there are some important things to be aware of.

We are talking about a person who will be going in and out of your apartment every day. If a stranger came up to you on the street and asked you for two sets of keys to your apartment, you would think they were crazy, but that is *exactly* what your dog walker will ask of you. You *cannot* be too cautious in selecting one.

Also, since the IRS began to crack down on waiters' unreported tips, dog walking has become one of the last truly great cash-only businesses, and *anyone* can print up a business card. Before you hand over your house keys and the end of your leash, be sure *who* you are giving those precious possessions to. Ask questions, and check references.

Right now the going rate seems to range from eight to fifteen dollars for a half-hour walk and twelve to twenty for an hour.

If the prospective dog walker starts to pull attitude, acts offended at your inquiries, or tries to intimidate you, you are not dealing with a professional. A professional New York dog walker will build a reputation in a neighborhood over the course of years, and will be happy to supply you with references. Maybe you'll hook up with someone really great who's just starting out—even the established walkers had "first clients." Just be very careful. If the dog walker comes from one of the bonded and insured pet-sitting services, it's much easier to relax and trust him/her.

Group or Pack Walks

Some dog-walking services offer group rather than individual walks. Group walks are generally a little less expensive than individual ones. Some dogs love the daily hurly-burly interaction with many canine buddies, while others might feel overwhelmed and stressed. If you do sign your dog up for group walks, be sure that the walker has at least one other partner so that the dogs are never left unattended. Sometimes group walkers will have to leave the dogs they have already picked up tied to a meter or a lamppost while fetching the other "walkees." During this time the unattended dogs are liable to be stolen or harmed. Be sure your questions are satisfactorily answered in this regard.

Finding a Dog Walker

The best ways to find reliable dog walkers are through one of the pet-sitting services or discovering one in your neighborhood with proven credentials and many satisfied customers. These people are a little harder to find, but your veterinarian, or word of mouth around your dog group, can put you on the right track. I guarantee that if you start asking dog folks in the park or on the street, you'll be given a lead on a good neighborhood walker. Many times, people opening a dog-walking service will begin by posting flyers on lampposts or at the local pet shop. These folks are rarely bonded or insured, so they offer you little protection or recourse when a problem arises. Use caution, and all your New York savvy, before handing your house keys over to a stranger.

Once you have settled on your dog walker, be sure all the terms are clear. Remember:

•The dog walker should have all of your contact numbers, your vet's phone number, and the number of a friend in the neighborhood.

•Be specific about your expectations. If you make your dog heel and sit at all curbs, then so should the walker. If you want the dog cleaned or dried off before being let in the house in inclement weather, then mention it and provide a towel or rag. If you don't want your dog getting any treats, say so.

•Let the walker know what he or she can expect from your dog. Is she aggressive or shy? Does she bark at tall people in hats? Does she grab and swallow in one gulp garbage she finds on the street? Is she afraid of subway grates, or of walking on those metal sheets that make up the entry to a thousand New York cellars?

Once the system is working, you may never cross paths with your dog walker. Keep tabs on the situation by periodically phoning the walker to ask how things are going. REMEMBER, YOUR DOG IS NOT GOING TO TELL YOU IF THINGS AREN'T GOING WELL! KEEP IN TOUCH WITH YOUR WALKER!

Just as taxis provide the convenience of getting about without the nuisance of keeping a car, hiring a dog walker is one of the *wonderful luxuries* of New York City living. Choose your dog walker wisely—then enjoy the peace of mind.

Pet-Sitting

The word *sitter* conjures up the image of a bored teenager watching TV and chatting on the phone while your dog chews through the baseboards. For this reason, pet-sitters often prefer to call themselves "in-home pet-care providers." The services they offer are ideally suited to the needs of a busy New Yorker who may be called away at any time on business (or pleasure).

Mr. Armstrong and Smokey

When a taxi jumped the curb in front of Tiffany's on Fifth Avenue last spring, two bystanders were injured. In the hospital, one received four get-well cards and a handful of visitors. The other got three to four hundred phone calls of concern a day and nearly as many letters and cards containing hundreds of dollars to ensure that he was taken care of. The first victim was an older blind man; the second, his black Lab guide dog, Smokey.

You might have seen Thomas Armstrong and Smokey on Fifth Avenue selling pencils. Mr. Armstrong said he didn't even hear the cab coming, but it mowed into them, breaking his leg, and pinning the terrified Smokey, who was blinded in the crash, under the front of the cab. New Yorkers lifted the cab off the pair and they were rushed to their respective hospitals—Mr. Armstrong to Bellevue and Smokey to the Animal Medical Center, where the veterinarians were able to restore some of his vision.

As they both recuperated, the cards and letters, many with donations, kept pouring in for Smokey. A Smokey-Get-Well Fund was established. After paying Smokey's medical expenses, the fund now offsets the costs of the free medical care the AMC has always provided to guide and service dogs.

Mr. Armstrong didn't seem to feel slighted by the outpouring of affection for his dog, but rather, honored. "I know people like dogs," he told a reporter, "but to write him letters an' all like that, makes me feel so good, because he's such a good dog."

In most pet-sitting arrangements, your dog is cared for in the security of her own home. When you go away she's *already* stressed by your absence, and the strange environment of a kennel can make things worse. In contrast, an in-home pet-care provider stops by several times a day to take your dog out and feed and spend time with her without the stress of a foreign environment.

This way, you can leave town knowing that your darling is in professional hands. Also, having your dog remain in your apartment and having someone stop in regularly keeps the burglars away. Sometimes you can even arrange for the pet-sitter to bring in the papers or mail and turn on the lights at night.

As I've mentioned, pet-sitting services can also supply you with a dog walker. Once again, sitting and walking include a stranger having access to your home—and, an even more precious possession, your dog. You *cannot* be too careful when screening and hiring an in-home pet-care provider or dog walker.

In an attempt to standardize the burgeoning industry, **Carol Tomaszewski** founded the **National Association of Professional Pet Sitters (NAPPS)** in 1985. NAPPS provides members with accreditation and liability and bonding insurance, and has set forth a code of ethics. It also provides a mentoring program for people getting started in the business.

Carol counsels dog owners looking to hire a pet-sitter who is not a member of NAPPS to be very careful. These are some of the guideline questions Carol suggests you pose to a prospective pet-sitter or dog walker:

- Are they bonded? (You may not feel comfortable asking if they have a police record, so this will suffice.)

- Do they have commercial liability insurance? (Remember, this person will be in your home and should have insurance just as your kitchen contractor would.)

- Will they provide you with references *you can easily check?*

- How long have they been in business?

In turn, your pet-sitter or dog walker should:

- Visit you beforehand to get detailed information regarding how long you will be gone and what you expect for your pet's care: feeding and walking schedule; vet's location and phone number; emergency contact numbers; what rules—if any—should be enforced (dogs have a particular genius for telling the sitter that they *really are* allowed on the furniture!); which dogs in the neighborhood you let your dog play with and which ones you avoid.

- Offer you a contract spelling out fees and services rendered.

• Assure you of contingency plans should bad weather or sickness delay the sitter.

• Seem comfortable and confident with your pet.

You can get more information regarding pet-sitting by contacting the **National Association of Professional Pet Sitters,** 1200 G Street, NW, Suite 760, Washington, DC 20005, 202-393-3317. NAAPS also offers a pet-sitter referral number, 800-296-PETS, where they will suggest pet-sitters in your area code.

Please don't make the mistake that many people have made by hiring a person who does not satisfy *all* of these points. *Anyone* can go to the nearest copy shop and have business cards printed up for five dollars. People have trusted their pooches to thieves impersonating pet-sitters, and have returned home from vacation to find an empty apartment—and no dog. You are a New Yorker! Use your street smarts!

Here is a list of businesses in New York that provide pet-sitting and dog walking:

MANHATTAN

Doggie/Kitty Nanny, 516 East 81st Street, 212-249-0877

Doggie Vacation, 212-861-8404

Family Affair Pet Care, 446 East 86th Street, 212-249-0839

Furry Tails, 212-938-TAIL (serves the Upper East Side *only*, 60th to 90th streets)

Noah's Ark Pet Care, 4416 6th Avenue, Brooklyn, 212-255-8939

Pet Patrol, 106 Greenwich Street, 212-924-6319

Pet Care Network, 251 East 32nd Street, 212-889-0756

Pet Get-Away, Third Avenue at 91st Street, 212-534-7924

Puddles Pet Service, 223 East 89th Street, 212-410-7338

Urban Animal, 212-969-8506

BROOKLYN

City Critters, 138 Remsen Street, 718-834-1777

Pet Patrol (serves Brooklyn Heights and Park Slope), 212-924-6319

Noah's Ark Pet Care (serves Manhattan also), 4416 6th Avenue, 212-255-8939

QUEENS

Critter Care, 71-31 Park Drive East, Flushing, 718-263-3770

Doggie Day Care

Doggie day care? Why not! While you're at work, why should your beloved pet languish at home? Why not send him to a doggie day care center? Children go to day care, why shouldn't dogs?

Naturally, we have the very best dog day care centers here in New York City. They provide fun, socialization, and exercise for otherwise apartment-bound dogs. It works this way: You drop your dog off in the morning on your way to work and pick her up on your way home. During the day she plays with pals, chews happily on the many toys strewn about the center, naps lazily on big comfortable furniture, has a snack and lunch (if you wish), snuggles in bed with other dogs and a human staff member, watching videos (reportedly *101 Dalmatians*, *The Incredible Journey*, and *Milo & Otis* are favorites!), and otherwise enjoys herself. Now that's the life!

Doggie day care is a *great* alternative, especially if your conscience nags you about the amount of free time you spend with your dog!

Another benefit to doggie day care is overnight or long-term boarding. You can leave your dog at the center whenever you need to. Lucy Scott, the *CBS News* producer, uses the West Side doggie day care center Canine Country as practically an annex to her apartment. Her greyhound, Annie, is *completely* comfortable there, and Lucy can drop her off on a moment's notice. If she

Alan Smith and his boxer, Buster, are homeless. Despite the difficult circumstances, Alan takes excellent care of Buster, and as gentle as he is loyal, Buster takes great responsibility for their life together. They are never apart, except on nights when the weather forces Alan into a shelter. Because dogs are not allowed in New York City shelters, Alan has an arrangement with a permanent pet-sitter who takes Buster on cold or wet nights. Credit: Deb Loven gets back to New York from a long assignment late in the evening, she can call Canine Country from the airport and pick Annie up on the way home.

Aside from the day care centers listed below, many grooming shops will accommodate "regular customers" in an informal day care setup. Why not let your dog be the "official greeter" at his favorite groomers? He'll be as eager to get to "work" bright and early every day as you are! Ask your groomer if some arrangement can be made.

Prices generally range from twenty to thirty dollars a day for day care, with added charges for pickup and delivery, grooming, and overnight boarding.

Here are some of the doggie day care centers in Manhattan that also offer twenty-four-hour boarding:

Canine Country, 207 West 75th Street (between Broadway and Amsterdam), 212-877-7777
In the same building as the Ansonia Veterinary, and A Cut Above dog-grooming salon, so your dog has access to those services as well. Big playroom for fun and exercise.

The Yuppie Puppy, 274 West 86th Street (between Broadway and West End Avenue), 212-877-2747
Offers a backyard with a swimming pool for summer fun and frolic. Big playroom; grooming done as well. Great place!

The Paws Inn, 370 West 35th Street (between 8th and 9th avenues), 212-736-7297
Big play zone with sloppy dog-friendly furniture. Upstairs "bedroom" where lots of snuggling and "Lassie" rerun watching goes on.

The Paws Inn (Chelsea), 189 Ninth Avenue (between 21st and 22nd streets), 212-645-7297
Twenty-four-hour day care. Offers grooming as well.

No Standing Anytime, 414 East 73rd Street (between 1st and York avenues), 212-472-0694
Picture the set of the Children's Television Workshop for dogs! Serious playtime fun to be had here! Offers a "school bus" to day care, pickup and delivery

service, and veterinary supervision by the Center for
Veterinary Care.

No Standing 2—Chelsea, 29th Street (between 10th and 11th avenues), 212-472-0694

Light! Space! Windows! The phenomenal 5,000-
square-foot new "downtown version" of No Standing
Anytime. Still offers the same great services, plus large
dog boarding and wonderful indoor training center.

Naturally, there are limitations to doggie day care. Some
dogs may not be comfortable in the environment, and day care is
not an option if your pet is very dog-aggressive, because he will
be expected to play nicely with the others. To monitor this, the
centers each have screening sessions to make sure your dog will
fit into the group.

Also, doggie day care is expensive. The current NYC rates
are between twenty and thirty dollars, with extra charges for special services like grooming, extra walking, and training. However, the cost is comparable to having a walker take your dog out
twice a day. The twenty-four-hour boarding rate is another added
charge, but is about the same as having a pet-sitter.

Boarding Your Dog

For a long stay, it is usually slightly less expensive to send your
dog away to a boarding kennel than to arrange for a pet-sitter or
dog day care, even with the kennel's pickup and delivery charge.

Remember, it is impossible to monitor what happens to your
dog when she is sent away to a kennel. For this reason you must
be sure you are sending your dog away to a reputable establishment. Make sure the business is a member of the American
Boarding Kennel Association, which monitors and sanctions its
members. You might also want to check with the local Better
Business Bureau or veterinarians in the area.

In any boarding situation, be sure that you are comfortable
with the veterinarian the establishment uses or have made it
clear that you want your own veterinarian to be called. Also supply them with the phone number of a friend or relative who may
be reached in case of an emergency if you are unavailable.

Check to see which dog food they serve. It is better to send your dog along with a supply of his own food—for gastric continuity—as well as his favorite toys and his bed or the blanket he sleeps on. If your dog is on any medication, include enough of it for the entire stay, with specific instructions as to how and when it is to be administered.

When your dog goes to a kennel, he will be housed either inside or in an indoor/outdoor run. He will be expected to relieve himself in an inconspicuous corner of his indoor space or outside in the run. But some dogs don't catch on. They consider the run part of the "house" and the outside portion the "patio," and they refuse to go. This is a problem. Kennel personnel are *supposed* to monitor the situation and leash-relieve these dogs. However, even at the best place, on a busy weekend the staff might *not* notice that your dog hasn't gone for two days and has a bladder the size of a football. Just to be safe, I suggest you pay the few dollars a day extra to have someone walk your dog.

Any boarding establishment will require that your dog be current with the major immunization shots: DHLP (distemper and hepatitis), parvovirus, rabies, and usually bordetella—commonly known as kennel cough. You will need to show written proof, which you can easily get from your vet's office.

Some boarding kennels offer "enhanced" services and call

ALL Rawhide Is Not Created Equal!

Does your dog love to chew on rawhide? Do you indulge him in knots and rings, thinking that he's safe gnawing on the leather? Think again. The *only* rawhide that is safe for dogs to chew on—and ingest—is the very thickest, whitest rawhide made from hides tanned in the U.S.A. Here, strict guidelines govern anything produced to be ingested by humans or animals, so hides for use in rawhide chews are free of chemicals or poisonous elements like lead and arsenic compounds. They are also of a thicker or heavier weight than imported rawhide. Only very heavy rawhide has the fiber to pass cleanly through your dog's system. Thin leather, cheaply tanned, can become slimy and stick in your dog's digestive system, where digestive enzymes may leach harmful chemicals from the leather. Only buy heavy, white, U.S.–made rawhide. When you see the thin brownish yellow stuff in the supermarket, walk on by.

themselves dog bed and breakfasts or dog lodges. Along with doggie day care, the concept of "dog hotels" has added a personal, or anthropomorphic, touch to canine care. By attempting to make the atmosphere more like home—with private "suites" or apartments—dog hotels bridge the gap between a pet-sitting arrangement and a traditional boarding kennel. Generally they cost a little more, but while you're enjoying a vacation at Canyon Ranch, your guilty conscience is eased by picturing your abandoned pet in the Versailles Suite of a dog hotel, watching her color TV from the luxury of her brass bed.

More traditional boarding kennels are usually equipped with individual indoor/outdoor runs, meaning four- or five-foot-square fenced areas, generally with a bed and running water. These connect by a door to a longer five by twenty-five feet or so outside area. The dogs can go in and out during the day but are closed inside at night. Frequently a large common play area is used for training, or free time, where dogs can socialize.

All the following establishments service New York City dogs by offering daily or biweekly pickup and delivery to and from your home. Grooming, private walking, extra exercise time, veterinary services, and training are also available for added charges.

Here are some of the dog hotels, doggie bed and breakfasts, and excellent boarding kennels serving New York City:

Almost Home Kennels, Pudding Street, Putnam Valley, NY 10579, 914-528-3000
Newly renovated facilities with indoor/outdoor runs. Canine playground, fitness program, grooming, and training, as well as pickup/delivery, available at extra charges.

Doyles Pet Bed & Breakfast, Austin Road, Mahopac, NY 10541, 914-628-4460
Located on four wooded acres, near Lake Mahopac, daily boarding costs as little as $14 per day for a suite, up to $50 for the "cottage"(if you have multiple pets, this is a good choice).

Graceland Kennels, 46 Graceland Lane, Ossining, NY 10562, 914-726-6188
Oldest continuously operated kennel in the U.S. Features large indoor/outdoor runs. Graceland supplies

the same food and medicines your dog uses at no extra charge.

Malibu Pet Hotel, 107 Guy Lombardo Avenue, Freeport, NY 11520, 516-379-6040

Your pet has the option of staying in a "dormitory-style run" or an actual apartment with one of the trainers. Grooming and training are also available.

Northwind Kennels, Route 22, Bedford, NY 10560, 914-234-3771

A "four star" dog resort. This is a ten-acre facility with various suites and areas named for chic vacation spots: Aspen, St. Tropez, Rome, Cape Cod. The posh Versailles Suite features a brass bed, a telephone, and a color TV for your dog to enjoy (close to $50 a day)! Less posh suites/runs are also available. You receive a full report card of how your dog fared in your absence: eating, sleeping, disposition, and oral skills (barking). Biweekly pickup/delivery to the city.

Quinkawol, 46-28 Route 209, Accord, NY 12404, 914-687-7619

The kennel and training center of the talented trainer Sue Sternberg. The kennel features thirty-one indoor/outdoor runs, and lots of personal attention for canine guests.

Rambling Acres, 170 South Hope Chapel Road, Jackson, NJ 08572, 908-370-8628

A wonderful facility run by an Animal Medical Center staff member and her husband. Indoor/outdoor runs, excellent supervision and care, and transportation from New York City arranged by rendezvous at the AMC. Grooming also available.

Willow Pet Hotel, 1926 Deer Park Avenue, Deer Park, NY 11729, 516-667-8924

"The Wald-ARF of pet hotels." They have 125 indoor/outdoor runs, a full grooming salon, and a kitchen to cater to your pet's special needs. Enthusiastic, caring staff.

Woods End Kennels, 66 Woods End Road, Putnam Valley, NY 10579, 914-528-3211

On 130 acres. Indoor/outdoor runs or "suites," as

well as private luxury suites with color TV, plush bed, and private play space. Dogs in the luxury suites are hand-walked several times and given extra playtime with the staff. Grooming is available.

Armed with this information, I hope you'll be able to find someone to watch over your New York dog, whatever the circumstance! Remember, no matter how much time they spend with the walker, the pet-sitter, or at the luxury kennel, what they prize the most is the time spent with you!

Chapter 6

Training

Minding the Manners of Your New York Dog

And something else: Tereza accepted Karenin [her dog] for what he was; she did not try to make him over in her image; she agreed from the outset with his dog's life, did not wish to deprive him of it, did not envy him his secret intrigue. The reason she trained him was not to transform him . . . but to provide him with the elementary language that enabled them to communicate and live together.
        –Milan Kundera,
        The Unbearable Lightness of Being

Why does your dog need to be trained? Because when you got your dog, you took on the responsibility of bringing a member of a different species into your human society. How will your dog learn to behave properly in a community of humans rather than with other dogs? It is your responsibility to teach him. You must train him to live with you, offering guidance and rules *in a language he understands*.

Training your dog gives him the tools to operate in your society.

It's also easier than *your* having to learn to live in dog soci-

ety. As a human being, you are ill equipped to perceive the
world the way dogs do. Compared to a dog, you smell three million times less accurately; you are nearly deaf, hearing a fraction
of the range of sound waves that dogs do; and you are uselessly
squeamish about things you touch with your nose or tongue.
These handicaps would mean that you wouldn't "get" practically
anything that was going on in the dog pack. It would be much
more confusing than living with Kalahari Bushmen, or what your
ancestors may have experienced upon arriving in New York after
passing through Ellis Island.

If you were adopted by a canine pack and lived with them,
you would be pretty much in the dark most of the time about how
to behave. Some things you would understand—displays of
affection, power, fun, discipline, anxiety, competition, tension,
reassurance, sadness, and joy all translate pretty easily. But
since you don't speak dog language, you might miss the nuance
of the slightly raised lip, flattened ears, and low vocalization
meaning "If you come any closer to this bone, I will bite you."
Missing the warning, you would reach for the bone and get bitten.

By the same token, your new dog might not understand your
earnest speech ending with ". . . so, since the rugs are from my
grandmother, and we've just had the floors redone. If *you* will sit
by the door and whimper, Lola, then *I* will know you need to go
out." Well, you know the joke. Lola stares earnestly at you,
pricking up her ears at the sound of her name. You interpret this
as a sign that she has understood and has agreed.

Fifteen minutes later, Lola noses around for a place to go to
the bathroom. Of course *you* don't notice this subtle flurry of
activity, since you are expecting Lola to sit by the door and
whimper as previously agreed upon. She finds a spot to her liking—in the center of the living room, on the beige part of the
oriental. You feel betrayed and contractually violated. Since
negotiation has failed and another peace treaty is broken, you
resort to the only other thing you know. You stick her nose in the
mess and whack Lola with a rolled-up newspaper the way your
grandfather used to hit his old dog, Fred. Maybe that will work.
Fred was a pretty good dog.

The experience has left you feeling ashamed and disheart-
ened. In our "therapized" world, where everyone is learning how
to communicate and get their needs met, haven't we progressed
past the rolled-up newspaper?

Yes and no. Corporal punishment will always "work" to a certain extent with dogs, as it "worked" in getting children to learn in Dickens's novels. They learn, but the schoolmaster with the cane is always the villain. The children are affected more emotionally than intellectually, and there is no joy in the process.

What was your most exciting educational experience at school? Probably one in which the teacher seemed to "speak" directly to you, presenting the material in a way that was engaging and comprehensible. When you clearly understood what was expected of you, and found it stimulating, learning was a joy. Why should it be any different for a dog?

The best way to teach another creature anything is to use a shared understanding, or language, to convey a specific idea or desired behavior. Then you must *consistently* and *positively reinforce* the correct performance. Through training, you must give your dog the skills, behaviors, and boundaries to live with your pack. This is what the most successful trainers and dog owners do.

If you can see your dog as an individual, a sentient creature experiencing the world in ways that are often more complex than you do—a gust of wind tells your dog more about his environment than fifteen minutes of CNN tells you—*that's* the start. If you can give him the respect of taking the time to learn as much about him as he knows about you, then you're on the right track. After all, you and your dog have plenty in common. You share the same living space and are affected by the same weather and have the same moods. He knows when you're joyful and buoyant, usually joining in your enthusiasm with his play behavior. He knows when you're angry and thus knows to avoid you until things are resolved, or if he has a guilty conscience, *really* avoid you! He knows your work patterns, your sleep patterns, and what other people you like or dislike.

So what do you know about your dog? Is he exquisitely sound-sensitive? Does he react to loud noises on the street or shrink from an angry outburst? If you know this, then you've got a pretty easy communication tool at your disposal—your tone of voice! Does she live and breathe for her tennis ball? Then why not orient her learning around the joy she experiences playing ball? You've got a perfect reward for every positive behavior—a few minutes of ball play. Would she sell her soul for a dog treat? It sounds as if carefully using her food drive would "speak" best to her. If you begin to establish a base of knowledge about your dog, you can choose the most appropriate learning style for him or her.

Remember, each breed was designed for something, but not necessarily obedience training. Some breeds are more "trainable" than others—and some individuals within specific breeds are more receptive than others. So don't be surprised if your terrier spends puppy kindergarten class trying to rowdily engage the other pupils in play, while the Border collie puppy next to you is concentrating on his owner's every breath, attempting to anticipate and jump to the next command. The Border collie is obviously "easier" to train. This is not to say that the terrier can't become equally as obedient. He's just bored with class and ready for playtime. Rather than despairing and feeling that he is a hopeless prospect, recognize his shorter attention span and keep your terrier-training sessions brief and fun. Ultimately, he'll learn as much as the Border collie—you just have to find the approach that appeals to him.

"Trainability" is not a measure of intelligence. It is ridiculous to say that a dog is not intelligent because he is not easily trained. Obviously, intelligence encompasses many more things than the ability to follow human commands. I don't really see how humans are in the position to judge canine intelligence, since so much of canine perception—their ranges of visual, auditory, and aromatic cues, to start—are imperceptible to us.

Smoking and Your Dog

In case you were looking for another reason to quit, you should be aware of the effects of your cigarette smoking on your dog. A recent study at Colorado State University's College of Veterinary Medicine and Biological Sciences showed that inhaling secondhand smoke can seriously damage your dog's health. Dogs are as prone to cancers as humans are, and the study found that dogs with short or medium-length snouts whose owners smoke have a 50 percent greater risk of developing lung cancer.

Interestingly, longer-snouted breeds owned by smokers seem to have a normal risk of lung cancer but are more susceptible to nasal cancer. Long- or short-nosed, all dogs are affected by the harmful irritants and carcinogens that are by-products of smoking. Remember, your dog doesn't have a choice.

What Does Your New York Dog Need to Know?

To be fully integrated into their owners' lives, New York dogs need a host of skills and abilities. To start with, since New Yorkers walk a lot, she needs to be a *pleasant* strolling companion. The New York dog paces herself to her owner, swerving to avoid those open cellar doors and subway grates. She doesn't pull on the leash unless she's letting you know that there's a really cute person you might want to meet, with an equally cute dog, across the street.

The New York dog pauses before stepping off the curb and into the street, and sits or stands quietly with you, waiting for the light to change. At the ATM machine, she sits by you, not bothering the person in the next booth. She accompanies you into the corner deli *without* grabbing anything from the salad bar while your back is turned, and tucks her tail in so that other customers don't step on it. When you need to meet the coop board, your New York dog accompanies you, lying quietly by your side during the interview, showing what a pleasure she will be to have in the building. She rides placidly on Metro North up to the country for a weekend, charming everyone in her train car. She's as hip and sophisticated as her owner.

How do you train a dog to do all those things? Well, most New York dogs are doing them already. The marvelous socialization dogs soak up by just *living* here provides the groundwork. The rest is done by you, her caring owner, who seeks guidance from a knowledgeable trainer.

How to Choose the Best Training Method for Your Dog

Discover what interests your dog—Frisbees, treats, tennis balls, whatever—as well as what gets his attention and immediately conveys to him that you are serious—a stern tone of voice or a physical correction. Armed with this, you are in the best position to select a trainer, or training method, for yourself and your dog.

The training process is for your benefit as well as your dog's.

It is as important that *you* learn how to give consistent, comprehensible commands as it is for your dog to learn what they mean and how to obey them. You need as much, if not more, training as your dog.

So pick a trainer who "speaks" to both of you, not one whose approach seems either too namby-pamby or too military for your learning style. For the two of you to get the best results from a training program, you both need to be as comfortable as possible with the technique.

There are other considerations: Pick the time of day and the place where your dog is most mentally receptive to training. Does she become playful after eating, or does she like to lie down and digest? If she gets playful *après* dinner, try scheduling your training sessions following a meal. Is she too distracted by the squirrels and other dogs in the park to focus on you? Try working inside at first. Perhaps you can't concentrate at home because the phone is always ringing. Paying attention to these potential distractions can make a difference in the quality of your training time.

Books and Tapes

How-to training guides are available in book form as well as on videocassette. These usually consist of famous trainers escorting you through the process of their training methods. You can learn the basics from any of these manuals, but books and tapes can't monitor how you execute the commands. One advantage of having a professional observe you and your pet's work is to critique you as an owner/command-giver.

Sending Your Dog Away for Training

Many busy New Yorkers choose to send their dogs away to live with, and be schooled by, professional dog trainers. If tennis camp helped improve their kid's game, why not send the dog away for lessons with the pro?

Well, it works, sort of. The professional, who already has an excellent rapport with dogs or he wouldn't be in business, takes the pet to a new place, away from the distractions and temptations of home, puts him into an organized training program, and usually gets pretty great results. Your dog's behavior problems fade to a distant unpleasant memory, and you get back a canine Rhodes scholar.

But what happens when normal life resumes? You barely have time to walk your pet, never mind spend a full hour on training. You still can't give the same command in the same way twice, so you sure don't speak dog like the trainer does. And your dog is back in his familiar environment, where he knows that his favorite fringe on the living room drapes tastes great.

Since *you* were not involved in the training process, you have missed building the bond that grows with your dog as you work and learn together. You also missed the very crucial *learning process*. You and your dog don't work as a *team*, rather, you are given operating instructions. Aside from the two or three hours of directions you get when your dog is returned, *you* have not learned anything about communicating with him. You can buy a computer and load it with software, and if you consistently use the right commands the program will always work. Paying a professional to train your dog is not as straightforward. Independent, free-thinking creatures cannot be expected to perform mechanically. You are better served in establishing the bond with your dog yourself and learning *with him* so that you are prepared when he behaves like a dog, not a computer.

Sending your pet away to be trained gets you a beautifully educated dog. Why not just keep the dog at home and become a beautifully educated owner?

Finding a Trainer

Your options for selecting a training program include: group obedience classes run at a center or in one of the parks; a private trainer who will come to your home and work one-on-one with you and your dog; and canine behaviorists who deal with the more complex issues of dogs with chronic problems. Since your veterinarian is familiar with you and your dog, he will probably be able to suggest a trainer to you. If you have a few choices already, your vet's advice can help you narrow down the choices.

Here are some tips for identifying the *kind* of training you and your dog need, and where to get access to the professionals to guide you.

The ASPCA Helpline

The **ASPCA's Companion Animal Services Behavior Helpline,** 212-876-7700, ext. HELP (4357) is open Monday through Friday from 1:00 to 5:00 P.M. (they will return calls left on their voice mail if you call at other times). This wonderful, free service offers you the chance to speak with a professional who will listen to your problems or concerns and give you advice or refer you to someone who can. If you are looking for a trainer, they will ask you to describe your dog—is he shy, aggressive, a ball player, et cetera—and what your goals are—basic obedience or an AKC title—then make suggestions from a long and proven list of professionals. The help line only recommends excellent, proven trainers, so you can trust their counsel. We New Yorkers are *very* lucky indeed to have such an excellent service at our fingertips.

American Dog Trainers Network

Another free help line is the **American Dog Trainers Network,** 212-727-7257. It primarily refers dog owners in search of guidance to trainers who are members of the Society of North American Dog Trainers. Founded in 1987 in an attempt to standardize the many individuals calling themselves "dog trainers," the society puts prospective members through a stringent screening and testing process. If accepted into the society, a trainer will have proven his or her knowledge of, and effectiveness with, dogs. As members, they must uphold the society's code of ethics, encompassing the use of humane training techniques, truth in advertising (an attempt on the part of the society to cut down on the many false "guaranteed techniques" and "secret methods" advertised in many Yellow Pages ads), a fair and appropriate fee base, and general professional deportment.

When dealing with a member of the society, you can be assured that you have a professional on your hands who will work effectively with your dog. You can also contact the **Society of North American Dog Trainers (SNADT)** directly for more information about their program at 212-243-7862.

Group Classes

The most popular way to educate yourself, and train your dog, is to enroll in a group obedience class. Generally, the trainer in charge of the program will meet with you ahead of time to assess your needs and goals. If you feel comfortable with her approach, like the rapport established with your dog, and think that you *both* can learn from her, she will suggest a class appropriate for your level and purpose.

A typical class meets once a week for six to ten weeks. There will be other owners and dogs, all at about your level, all confronting the same sorts of problems. As well as learning how to handle and educate your dog, you will enjoy support from the other owners and will be able to consult your trainer about difficulties you may be experiencing outside the class.

One unbeatable benefit to working with your dog in a group setting is that he or she learns to focus on you despite distractions. The private trainer can come to your home, and your dog can be a perfect angel, but get him on the street and he reverts to a perfect devil. He must learn to concentrate on you, no matter what. Believe me, the nature of a group setting provides plenty of distractions!

Puppy kindergarten is the way to start, and you can begin as soon as your puppy has all her shots (twelve weeks). Puppy class is where you build the foundation of your relationship with your pet. Body handling, learning to walk on a leash, sit, come, and sometimes down and stay are included depending on the age and aptitude of the class members. Although it is important to get your pup started, you can't expect too much from him. House training itself is a big enough concept for a little head with a very short attention span. A puppy's brain is not even completely developed until he is seven weeks old—and sometimes it seems not until a year or two! Be sensitive to how many new ideas you present to your baby. Keep track of how long he

Trainer Terry Firth and Ollie "the Wonderdog" in Brooklyn's Prospect Park, performing one of Ollie's many tricks with the help (and bicycle) of young Andre Raymond. An untrained puppy, Ollie was Terry's first client when he brought his dog-training business to New York four years ago. Now they perform frequently at schools and events. Credit: Deb Loven can concentrate so that your training remains fun, not a chore.

I made this mistake with my dog Pally. With obedience champions all over his pedigree, I was sure that he would be a star. I had him in class promptly the first day after his shots, and we worked diligently on a daily basis. Heel! Sit! Stay! He must have felt as though he had been born into the French foreign legion. My friend Jan's dog, Cammie, had gotten her first obedience title, a C.D., at nine months. I was sure I could match that with Pally.

Luckily for Pal, another litter came along, and I was distracted enough to give him a few months off. When we resumed, he was just over a year old. In the time off, he had matured mentally and was now able to contextualize what I asked of him. He could concentrate longer, carry ideas over from one exercise to the next, and most important, relax into the exercises so that he enjoyed them. It was the difference between trying to teach long division to a first-grader and a fifth-grader. I had been a dope.

Get your puppy into class, get the support and guidance you need, but make sure he is having fun. Remember, as individuals, dogs learn and grow at different rates. Be responsive to your dog's abilities and maturity level.

Basic training for dogs six months and older usually consists of heel, sit, stay, come, and down. You may have covered these commands in puppy kindergarten, but it doesn't hurt to review. Intermediate training begins with off-leash heeling, longer stays, and recalls. If you progress through to advanced levels, you might consider working toward an obedience degree. In chapter seven, the kinds of obedience competitions are discussed.

Here are some of the businesses offering group training classes, private counseling, and help for the dog owner in distress:

ASPCA, 424 East 92nd Street, New York, NY 10128, 212-876-7700, ext. 4357

The ASPCA runs several training classes at their center on East 92nd Street. Their courses run for eight weeks, and they offer puppy kindergarten, several levels of obedience, a fun and games class, and a visiting dog program—an advanced training program for those who wish to do volunteer work in schools, hospitals, and convalescent homes with their dogs. Discounts are given to dogs adopted from the ASPCA. A great resource!

The Bide-A-Wee Home Association, 410 East 38th Street, New York, NY 10016, 212-532-4455

Private and group classes are offered at their center. Their rates are reasonable (for New York), and there is an added discount for dogs adopted from Bide-A-Wee.

CITYDOG, 158 West 23rd Street, New York, NY 10011, 212-255-3618

Their center, wonderfully decorated with antique dog photos and literature, offers a permanent training space for their many classes. They also go to the park, weather permitting. Cover dog, Daisy, was trained there with great results!

Fieldston Dogs Inc., 3476 Bailey Avenue, Bronx, NY 10463, 718-796-4541

Bash Dibra, famous trainer/author, offers group classes in Van Cortlandt Park, as well as personal counseling and "TV training" classes in Manhattan.

Follow My Lead, 316 West 83rd Street, New York, NY 10024, 212-877-0100

Excellent program offering several types of group classes, in-home instruction, problem solving, and consultations. Groups held indoors as well as in the park. Services all boroughs. Wonderful reputation.

No Standing Anytime, 414 East 73rd Street (between 1st and York avenues), New York, NY 10021, 212-472-0694

No Standing 2—Chelsea, 29th Street (between 10th and 11th avenues), New York, NY, 212-472-0694

Group classes and private sessions held at both locations. Positive, effective approach.

Prospect Park Dog Training, Prospect Park, Brooklyn, NY, 718-788-3602

Group classes in Prospect Park under the direction of trainers Barbara Giella and Lori Sash-Gail. Especially good puppy kindergarten. Private sessions as well.

Vancouver Associates, 120 Riverside Drive, New York, NY 10023, 212-877-7116
Group classes in all phases of obedience, puppy kindergarten, socialization, and pet therapy. In-home and private consultations as well.

Private Trainers/Consultants

Many dogs and their owners need more guidance and personal attention than is offered in a group class. Like a personal trainer who creates an exercise program to fulfill your specific needs, private dog trainers work one-on-one with their clients. They come to your home at your convenience, designing a program for your goals and lifestyle. They are also able to help you with short-term problems like housebreaking, chewing, or preparing your dog to meet a coop board. Since you and your dog have the trainer's undivided attention, progress is swift. Be sure that the

Why Not Join an Obedience Club?

Some really wonderful resources are the **Staten Island Companion Dog Training Club,** Immanuel Lutheran Church, 2018 Richmond Avenue, Staten Island, NY 10314, 718-761-8048; the **Port Chester Obedience Club,** 230 Ferris Avenue, White Plains, NY 10603, 914-946-0308; and **The Dog Obedience Club of South Nassau,** American Legion Hall, 197 Maple Avenue, Rockville Center, NY 11570, 516-766-9740 (call Monday and Tuesday evenings, 6:30 to 9:00 P.M.). These obedience clubs offer classes in obedience for pleasure and competition. Since they are nonprofit clubs, their rates are roughly one-fourth to one-third the price of comparable work in the city. You also have the benefit and fun of meeting and working with people who show their dogs all the time. They also sponsor many events themselves. Of course, transportation is an issue, but many club members commute from the city. Call them, because there is always the possibility of carpooling.

trainer also works with both of you outside, in the environment where problems typically occur. If your dog lunges uncontrollably at squirrels in the park, then be sure that enough time is spent with the trainer *in the park* so that the problem is solved. A private trainer is a wonderful way for the busy New Yorker to educate himself and his dog.

All of the companies listed offering group obedience classes also send trainers to work with you privately. Additional private trainers include:

Stephen Diller, 914-526-2429

An excellent motivational trainer.

Debbie Feliciani, 516-585-7098

Positive, fun approach, based in Long Island, but will travel to the city for special clients.

Terry Firth, 718-252-2998

Terry has an almost magical rapport with canines. He can train any dog, but is particularly gifted with the big, challenging ones who might be a little too strong or a little too smart for other trainers. Private sessions all over the city, protection work as well as obedience.

Robin Kovary, Canine Companion, 161 West 4th Street, #2, New York, NY 10014, 212-243-5460

Sensitive, effective approach, excellent with puppies. Robin is an accomplished trainer and dog writer who also runs the Canine Resource and Referral Hotline, so she has her finger on the pulse of "what's up with dogs" in New York City. Private and semiprivate sessions available. Certified Canine Good Citizen Evaluator and Pet Therapy Instructor/Coordinator. Discounts for adopted and rescued dogs.

Michele Siegel, 718-829-8905

Private sessions primarily in the Bronx. Occasional group classes as well.

Sue Sternberg, Quinkawol, 46-28 Route 209, Accord, NY 12404, 914-687-7619

Excellent trainer with a great reputation. Does private sessions in New York City and group classes at Quinkawol in Accord, NY.

The U.S. Customs New York Region Canine Enforcement Program

There are some pretty talented noses working at Kennedy International Airport to keep illegal narcotics out of New York. These canine superstars detect drugs concealed by traffickers in luggage, cargo, parcels, and aircraft, and carried bodily by passengers. In the past ten years alone, New York's Canine Teams of drug-sniffing dogs, and their Enforcement Officer partners, have seized over a quarter of a million pounds of marijuana, nearly fifty thousand pounds of hashish, more than seven hundred pounds of heroin, thirty thousand pounds of cocaine, and over $75,000,000 in currency.

A dog's sense of smell is roughly two million times more acute than our own. They experience smell the way we experience vision. For example, if a gram of cocaine is hidden in a pound of coffee, inside a round of stinky Roquefort cheese, or floating in a barrel of cod-liver oil, the dog does not have to sort through the layers of smells. He experiences a scent "picture," rather like the design of a bull's-eye, with the cocaine at the center and all the other smells as rings around it.

There are many misperceptions about the way drug dogs are trained. Some people actually think that the dogs are given the drugs to acquire a taste for them. This is ridiculous. But how do you teach a dog to look for cocaine? By channeling the dog's most natural instinct—his love of play. Canine candidates for narcotics detection work are usually sporting or working breeds who are confident, energetic, enthusiastic, and "demonstrate an intense desire to retrieve any thrown object."

Training begins with the dogs playing tug and fetch with their handlers. Instead of a ball, a towel is used, and the dogs quickly begin to see towels as their favorite toys. Soon the game of hide-and-seek with the towel is introduced and distinct artificial scents are added to the neutral-smelling terry cloth. The dogs begin to use their noses to find their toy, learning that their towel can smell different ways. They also learn to signal their handler of the towel's presence, and when the handler uncovers it, they are rewarded. The entire thing is one big game.

What the dogs do not understand is that the scents added to their towels that they have learned to identify are imitations of the fragrance of different narcotics. When a working narcotics dog smells his "towel" hidden inside a piece of luggage on a baggage cart at JFK and scratches on the bag, telling his handler where it is, he has actually located a cache of illegal drugs. The towel is absent, but the dog is rewarded just the same.

Ultimately, the game changes from "find the towel" to "find the thing which smells like the towel." The ability of the canines to discern the scent is so great that they are rarely foiled.

Ivan Kovich, 212-682-6770 (days), 718-373-7512 (evenings)
A member of the Society of North American Dog Trainers, he is particularly effective with strong (physically and mentally) dogs. Protection training is offered as well as basic obedience.

A special mention must be made of **Vicki Hearne**'s work. A preeminent theorist and author of several brilliant books on the relationship between humans and animals (*Adam's Task: Calling Animals by Name, Bandit: Dossier of a Dangerous Dog, Animal Happiness*), she trains dogs—and their owners. Working with Vicki Hearne is serious business and involves commitment as well as getting up to Westbrook, Connecticut, regularly, but her rates are stunningly reasonable. She is a master trainer, behaviorist, poet, and philosopher. Working on your dog with her is akin to having Freud himself as your therapist.

Behaviorists

An animal behaviorist specializes in coping with the more complex issues of animal behavior that stretch beyond the boundaries of conventional obedience training or medical help. A canine behaviorist approaches problems in a different way. Let's say your dog chews. I don't mean a little chewing during teething, I mean obsessive, relentless, self-mutilative chewing, a compulsion from which he might injure himself by ingesting glass or metal. You have tried everything your trainer suggested—distracting him, correcting him, crating him—to no avail. Your vet has attacked the problem with drugs and hormones, without much success.

A behaviorist will approach the problem from a psychological perspective, using behavior modification techniques to prevent destructive or unwanted behavior and to encourage appropriate behaviors. These are not "dog shrinks," but serious professionals who will work positively with you and your dog to find solutions.

We are very fortunate in New York City to have access to **The Animal Behavior Consultants Inc.,** 2465 Stuart Street, Brooklyn, NY, 212-721-1231 or 718-891-4200. This marvelous practice includes Peter Borchelt, Ph.D., who is also on the staff of the Animal Medical Center; Linda Goodloe, Ph.D., and Valeda Slade, M.S. They offer a low-cost telephone help line and make house calls.

So get yourself, and your dog, into a training program. Whatever trainer or method you choose, be consistent! Remember, it will be challenging for you and your dog to learn this new "language." Be clear, be kind to your dog, and have a wonderful time learning and growing together.

Chapter 7

Go for It! Taking Your Training Beyond the Basics

Fun Programs, Competitions, and Groups to Get Involved With

O nce you and your dog have the training tools to live together in relative harmony, you may find that you want to continue working to a more professional level. The time spent on training will build a deeper, more satisfying bond between you and your dog. I know, this is starting to sound like a book on relationships . . . well, it is, you're just dealing cross-species! If you have the time and energy, doing additional training with your dog can be terrifically rewarding.

Your options for pursuing "higher education" with your dog include: American Kennel Club programs like the Canine Good Citizen test; competitive obedience through the various breed registries; tracking and working competitions; pet therapy programs; search and rescue clubs; *Schutzhund*; competitive police work; recreational activities like lure coursing and Frisbee competitions. So where do you want to begin?

Canine Good Citizens

The American Kennel Club established the **Canine Good Citizen** test to promote and encourage responsible dog ownership. Open to mixed breeds as well as purebred dogs, the CGC is a noncompetitive certification program. The test is comprised of ten exercises that evaluate your dog's obedience, responsiveness, and general deportment. Exercises include a knowledge of basic obedience commands as well as several temperament evaluation tests—walking calmly through a crowd, being approached and petted by a stranger, encountering a strange dog, reacting to distractions, and being left alone. All dogs who pass receive an official AKC Canine Good Citizen Certificate (we have Serena's up on the refrigerator!), a personalized CGC ID tag, and a wallet card for you.

Frequently, training groups will offer classes specifically geared toward the CGC test. If you sign up for a basic obedience class and want to try for CGC, inform your instructor, and he or she should be able to guide you with exercises "grooming" you for the test. In New York City, most Canine Good Citizen tests are administered by the ASPCA. You can get information by calling their Companion Animal Services at 212-876-7700. You may also contact **The American Kennel Club,** Attention: Canine Good Citizen Program, 5580 Centerview Drive, Suite 200, Raleigh, NC 27606.

Therapy Dogs

What could be more rewarding than sharing the love and happiness your dog provides with someone confined to a nursing or convalescent home? A therapy dog program offers you this chance. Once you are certified and registered with one of the therapy dog organizations, you and your dog will be able to regularly visit hospitals, homes, and special education programs at schools, spreading good cheer or just supplying someone with a furry neck to hug and a kiss on the cheek (that would be your *dog*, of course, doing the kissing).

Certifying your dog for therapy work includes taking the Canine Good Citizen test, but with elements that reflect what your dog might encounter in a nursing home or hospital. There is generally a wheelchair your dog must approach and stay near without fear, a food distraction—how would you feel if your golden entered a patient's room and coolly stole the sandwich off his tray?—and other potential distractions like noisy children, canes, and walkers. Obviously, you should acclimate your dog to some of these potential distractions before the test, and you can even prepare, as you would for the Canine Good Citizen test, with a private trainer or group. In New York City the experts on therapy dog work are **Robin Kovary,** a trainer and Pet-Assisted Therapy evaluator, 212-243-5460, and the **ASPCA's Companion Animal Services,** 212-876-7700. You can also receive information from the governing bodies, **The Delta Society,** 321 Burnett Avenue South, 3rd floor, Renton, WA 98055, 206-226-7357, **Therapy Dogs Incorporated,** 2416 East Fox Farm Road, Cheyenne, WY 82007, 307-638-3223, and **Therapy Dogs International,** 260 Fox Chase Road, Chester, NJ 07930.

The Animal Medical Center has a wonderful **Pet Outreach Program** involving qualified pet owners and their dogs (and cats) visiting various nursing homes, halfway houses, and prisons in the metropolitan area. Typically, volunteers and their pets accompany a coordinator from the Pet Outreach Program to the facility and spend an hour or two interacting with the residents.

Visits to the Adolescent Detention Facility of Riker's Island Correctional Facility have been among the most successful pet outreach initiatives. While interacting with the pets, the young inmates are able to relax, dropping their bravura postures, expressing affection, and socializing in a warm atmosphere. Even the guards look forward to the Pet Outreach Program visits because the dogs bring out an entirely different side of the "kids" than they usually see. They report that the night following an evening visit, the usual fights between inmates rarely break out, making the guards' jobs a little easier. It's a great program! To get involved, contact the **Pet Outreach Coordinator** at the **Animal Medical Center,** 212-838-8100.

Diane Piselli, director of **Love Unlimited Pet Therapy Program,** 41-40 Union Street, #12G, Flushing, NY 11355, 718-

Robin Kovary and golden retriever therapy dog Sam visit the Village Nursing Home in Greenwich Village. Robin has done therapy work with several breeds of dog—including her own American Staffordshire terrier. She finds that the happiness and warmth that the dogs bring to those she visits make the hours of training and travel worthwhile. Credit: Petography

353-8252, runs a great program under the guidance of Therapy Dogs International. It's a network of volunteer pet therapy teams that visit facilities in New York City. If you are at all interested in this work, they can get you going.

Obedience Competitions

The America Kennel Club (AKC), the United Kennel Club (UKC), and the American Mixed Breed Obedience Registration (AMBOR) also sanction dog shows and matches in which you can compete in obedience on several levels. The matches are a smaller, less formal version of the shows, where you can practice under show conditions. The results are not counted toward any awards or titles. The shows are grander affairs, and the results count.

Your dog must be registered with one of these governing bodies to compete in their sanctioned events. I discuss dog registration in chapter one, but if you have any questions about your dog's status, check with the breeder who sold you your pup. If you received no registration information with your dog, or have a "Heinz 57," all is not lost! The **United Kennel Club (UKC),** 100 East Kilgore Road, Kalamazoo, MI 49001, 616-343-9020, accepts *pedigreeless* dogs to compete in obedience trials and hunting retriever trials under their "Limited Privilege Registration." The dogs must be spayed or neutered, and a photograph of your dog showing him to "look like a Lab" will be enough for him to be registered as such.

If your dog is a *very* merry mix, and shows no obvious ancestry, he can be registered with the **American Mixed Breed Obedience Registration (AMBOR),** 205 1st Street S.W., New Prague, MN 56071, 612-758-4598. Both registries sponsor obedience titles, non-obedience titles (like agility work), and many annual trophies and awards. Join the fun!

There are three successively more challenging obedience levels, with titles or degrees, which your dog can win. *Novice:* Companion Dog (C.D.) consists of six basic exercises: heel on leash, heel free, stand for examination, a long recall, long sit, and long down stay. *Open:* Companion Dog Excellent (C.D.X.) is seven exercises: heel free, drop to a down stay on a recall, retrieve an object, retrieve over a high jump, a broad jump, long

sit, and long down. *Utility:* Utility Dog (U.D.), the most challenging, is performed silently with the dog working from hand signals
rather than voice commands, and includes scent discrimination,
jumping, retrieving, and a group examination.

To earn an obedience degree, a dog must get three "legs" at
three separate dog shows. A "leg" is won if your dog obtains a
score of 170 or higher out of a possible 200 points, and more
than 50 percent credit on each exercise.

Sounds easy? Not! Blowing any single exercise costs you the
class, even though the rest of the performance might have been
flawless. It can be as nerve-racking as Olympic ice skating.

But obedience competitors are a dedicated group. I had a
girlfriend with a particularly clever husky named Boris. She had
trained this dog within an inch of his life so that Boris was performing the routine for the C.D. title in his sleep. Confident that
he would easily win his three legs in three successive shows, she
planned on kicking back and relaxing for the rest of the summer.

At the first show, Boris heeled perfectly, but when she com-
manded him to come to her on the recall, he looked mystified,
as though he had never heard the word *come* in his life. Zero
credit, one leg blown. They continued, and Boris did the other
exercises perfectly. All the next week they practiced recalls. At
the next show, he heeled on leash, came on the recall, but when
she took his leash off for the free heeling, Boris wandered out of
the ring to make friends with the dogs waiting on deck. She was
halfway through the heeling pattern before she realized that he
wasn't with her. Another leg blown. More off-leash heeling
practice all week. The third show brought perfect performances
in heeling and recall, but when the judge approached him for
the stand for examination, Boris threw himself on the ground
and rolled over to have his stomach scratched. No credit for the
stand, no leg.

This continued through June, and into July and August.
Every week she diligently trained Boris, paid the entry fees, and
schlepped to a show, and every weekend he found some new and
unpredictable way to get zero credit on at least one of the exercises. He would execute everything else flawlessly and would
never mess up in the same way twice. It was impossible to prepare for his "flunk of the day," and thus impossible to train
around the problem. The only thing for sure was that Boris
would flunk *something*.

At summer's end, when she and Boris had been to no less
than fifteen shows—yes, every weekend, plus the "Three Shows

in Three Days" long weekend in Vermont—without a single leg to show for their efforts, Boris finally broke her spirit. It was the last exercise, he had done everything else perfectly. His sits had been straight, his stand for examination solid as a rock, his recall like an arrow to the mark, his long sit composed and regal. I could see her thinking "Finally, we'll get one!"

Two minutes into the five-minute-long down stay, Boris's tail began to wag. Technically he was still lying down, but he began to inch imperceptibly toward her, his tail thumping. It was more like a wiggle than an actual crawl, and you had to look hard and note landmarks to see him covering ground, but he was soon a full body length out of line with the other dogs. When the judge called "Return to your dog" at the end of the five minutes, Boris had traversed the ring and lay at her feet, smiling up at her. Another zero.

What can you do with a dog like that? His sense of either whimsy or theater overrode his will to perform a routine he had done a million times. He had probably enjoyed all the attention and travel the summer had brought. Boris just couldn't resist creatively embellishing the prescribed routine. It was the entertainer in him. Impossible, unreasonable, completely Boris. She knelt down and gave him a hug.

If Boris's tale hasn't filled you with dread of the hidden "showman" in your dog, and if you and your dog find working together mutually enjoyable, I urge you to go farther with training. A working dog is a happy dog. Of course, some breeds, and individual "stars" within breeds, display more natural aptitude for different types of work—it is easier to prepare for and win a sheep-herding trial with a Border collie than with a Newfoundland—but all dogs can be channeled into something.

Entering obedience competitions and pursuing titles with your dog is very rewarding. The most natural way to become involved is to train with a professional or an obedience club. Clubs are not-for-profit and usually have a good trainer on board, as well as members who compete regularly themselves and have years of practical experience. Obedience clubs usually host seminars on canine topics, give obedience demonstrations in their communities, and have social events—there's *always* a doggie costume party at Halloween!

Accompany the club to shows and matches to see how you like the "scene." This is also a good way to introduce your pet to the dog show world before he is expected to perform in it. Since your dog is a New Yorker, after the initial excitement of car rides to the country, he will probably act very blasé about the whole production. After all, what is a dog show but an extended, organized play group?

Some great clubs in our area are:

Newtown Kennel Club
2 Tucktaway Lane
Danbury, CT 06810

Port Chester Obedience Club
230 Ferris Avenue
White Plains, NY 10603
914-946-0308

The Dog Obedience Club of South Nassau
American Legion Hall
197 Maple Avenue
Rockville Center, NY 11570
Call Monday and Tuesday evenings, 6:30 to 9:00 P.M.
516-766-9740

Staten Island Companion Dog Training Club
Immanuel Lutheran Church
2018 Richmond Avenue
Staten Island, NY 10314
718-761-8048

Tracking and Trialing

In addition to obedience competitions, The American Kennel Club sanctions tracking tests resulting in a Tracking Dog (T.D.) or Tracking Dog Excellent (T.D.X.) titles. Any breed may compete in tracking, following a scent over a prescribed course, and it's a wonderful way to use the amazing scenting ability your dog has. The only group in our area is the **Hudson Valley Tracking Club,** RD 5, Box 51, Wynantskill, NY 12198.

Field trials test the ability of the sporting breeds to continue to perform their original function. Hundreds of field trials are held all over the country each year. If you have purchased a puppy from a breeder who competes in trials, he or she will guide you. Should you decide to pursue your dog's inbred talents without a breeder's guidance, information is also available through the AKC and various breed clubs that sponsor competitions appropriate for their breed.

Schutzhund

The sport of *Schutzhund* (German for "protection dog") began at the end of the last century as a temperament and working ability test for the newly developed breed of German shepherd dogs. It grew to encompass other breeds as owners took interest in training their dogs in the discipline and competing against other owner/dog teams to earn degrees or titles.

Three elements compose *Schutzhund* work: tracking, obedience, and protection, and there are three levels of difficulty, *Schutzhund* I, *Schutzhund* II, and *Schutzhund* III. The difficulty of the requirements rises with each level, so that a trained *Schutzhund* III dog is capable of work roughly equivalent to that of a working police dog.

Although developed specifically for German shepherd dogs, *Schutzhund* work is performed today by many different breeds, the most popular being the classic working or protection breeds like Dobermans, rottweilers, giant schnauzers, Belgian Malanois, and boxers. In recent years there has been an influx of American Staffordshire terriers, as well as breeds you wouldn't immediately associate with police work, like Australian shepherds and Border collies. Any type of dog can be trained to do *Schutzhund* work, as long as they are physically strong enough to do the jumping and protection portions of the test.

Schutzhund work is serious business, for committed, talented handler/dog teams. It is not to be entered into casually and takes long hours of intensive work. Training for the protection component includes getting access to and channeling your dog's aggressive side. He must be able to defend you on command. This door to your dog's aggression is *not* one that you want to open unless you are prepared to take a lot of responsibility for it.

A fully trained *Schutzhund* dog is a complete companion— serene and obedient, able to follow the track of a child who has strayed or leap to the protection of his master. If you are interested in pursuing the discipline, the best way is to find a local *Schutzhund* club and begin attending their meetings and training sessions. You can find out more about the sport by contacting

United Schutzhund Clubs of America, 729 Lemay Ferry Road, St. Louis, MO 63125, the governing body in this country.

Search and Rescue

This is serious business, requiring commitment and some prior obedience work. Most important, it requires a communicative bond between you and your dog that is almost a private shared language. You will be able to tell your dog the scent he must follow and be able to "read" his body language and movements to help him in his quest. The point of all this, of course, is to find the lost baby, the disoriented person who has wandered away, or anyone else who has left a scent trail for your dog to follow. Search and rescue clubs typically get together to work every few weekends. It usually takes about a year and a half for you and your dog to reach proficiency (the dog is ready sooner, but you have a lot of compass reading and map work to master as well!).

The Ramapo Rescue Dog Association, 247 Airmount Avenue, Ramsey, NJ 07446, 914-469-4173, is a volunteer wilderness rescue service that trains in Bear Mountain State Park. They use only German shepherd dogs but are happy to train new dog/handler teams. If you have a shepherd and want to put that nose to use, give them a call. The **National Association for Search and Rescue,** P.O. Box 3709, Fairfax, VA 22308, 703-352-1349, can give you more general information.

Herding

If only we still had a flock in Central Park's Sheep Meadow! Yes, herding trials and herding instinct certification is all about making sheep, or ducks (or children if you've got toddlers around the house), go in the direction you and your herding dog (obviously, the collie breeds, the sheepdogs, the shepherds, the corgis, et cetera) want them to go. The Herding Instinct Certification is a noncompetitive test to evaluate your dog's innate herding ability even though he has had little or no formal experience in working stock. The competitive trials are for dogs with *lots* of formal training. Contact the AKC or the **American Herding Breed Association,** 1548 Victoria Way, Pacifica, CA 94044, for more information.

Lure Coursing

For all of you out there with retired racing greyhounds, Afghans, basenjis, borzois, or any of the other "sight hounds," *this is for you*! Lure coursing allows your dog to vent all that pent-up running/hunting drive he rarely gets to vent within the confines of the city. The dogs chase a strip of plastic, meant to represent prey, attached to nylon cord stretched in a series of turns and straightaways over a prescribed course, from 500 yards to over a mile long. Aside from taking your hound to the desert and setting him on some hapless jackrabbit, this may be the only time you see him at a full gallop, racing the wind pursuing game as his ancestors did for centuries. You can get more information about lure coursing from the **American Sight Hound Field Association,** 2234 Walnut Avenue, McKinnleyville, CA 95521.

Channeling All That Canine Energy: Agility Work

As we all know, dogs just love to jump over, crawl under, and clamber around on things. Agility courses, which are a combination of a doggie playground and an obstacle course, make the most of these "talents." You might have mistaken your dog's aptitude for agility work as an annoying habit when he jumped on the dining-room table after a leg of lamb. But working through the various jumps, tunnels, seesaws, and ramps builds your dog's trust and confidence in you, strengthening the bond you share. In competition, you race the clock to get through the course quickly and cleanly, but just running your dog through the obstacles without competing is fun for both of you. The **Port Chester Obedience Club,** 230 Ferris Avenue, White Plains, NY 10603, 914-946-0308, and **The Dog Obedience Club of**

South Nassau, American Legion Hall, 197 Maple Avenue, Rockville Center, NY 11570, 516-766-9740 (call Monday and Tuesday evenings, 6:30 to 9:00 P.M.), have added agility to the activities they offer. You can also contact the governing body, the **United States Dog Agility Association,** P.O. Box 850955, Richardson, TX 75085, 214-231-9700, and ask them for a list of clubs or events in your area.

Is Your Dog a Frisbee Dog?

Yes, what you thought of as a convenient way to exercise your dog has become a sport! There are rules and regulations, but Frisbee basically comes down to your dog performing jumping and retrieving tricks worthy of Michael Jordan or Baryshnikov. The Friskies company has really taken the sport on, sponsoring the annual Friskies Canine Frisbee Championship. The most famous canine Frisbee athlete was the purebred whippet, Ashley, owned and trained by Alex Stein (it is legend that Stein fed Ashley, from puppyhood, out of an upside-down Frisbee!). Stein has put out a manual for training your dog to be a Frisbee champ, which you can get, along with information about competitions, from **Friskies,** 800-423-3268, or write to: Friskies Competitions, 4060-D Peachtree Road, Suite 326, Atlanta, GA 30319. Excellent!

There's lots more to do with your dog than just walking around the block! Channeling his energy through an activity and getting the competitive juices flowing (for *both* of you!) can be a blast. So go for it!

The Beagle Brigade

Imagine you are in the crush of passengers retrieving luggage from an international flight at JFK or one of the other major international airports here in the States. One of your bags has arrived and when you look down, your gaze is met by the warm brown eyes of a beagle sitting at your feet next to your luggage. As you bend down to pet him, the beagle's handler, a U.S.

Department of Agriculture inspection officer, asks to look through your bags. You have just been busted by the Beagle Brigade.

Your infraction may be as innocent as an orange you threw in your bag to eat in the plane, but it is the job of APHIS, the Animal and Plant Health Inspection Service, to keep the foreign bug that might be hidden in your orange from entering the States. These officers, and the beagles that assist them, are the first line of defense against imported pests and diseases that could seriously damage American agriculture.

APHIS uses beagles because they have excellent noses, are usually raised in packs, so they remain calm in crowds and confusion, and are gentle and nonthreatening to the public. Rather than bark or scratch the bag when they detect something, the beagles are trained to simply sit down next to the suspect piece of luggage or container. This quiet statement on the dog's part alerts his handler, allowing the work of detecting prohibited fruits, plants, or meats to go on without interrupting most of the other passengers in the busy terminal.

Canine candidates for the Beagle Brigade are donated by private owners or breeders. During a twelve-week training period the dogs learn to respond by passively sitting when they smell citrus fruits, mango, beef, or pork. They are then matched with officers and placed at duty stations at different airports within the U.S. Because of their sensitivity to the smell of food, the beagles live in kennels, rather than at home with their human partners. A deep bond develops between the inspectors and their dogs (they have the option of keeping their beagle as a pet when the dog is retired) as the inspectors learn to "read" the slightest nuances of their dog's behavior when working. From the first four scents they learn in training, the working beagle's "scent vocabulary" quickly expands to encompass hundreds of different smells. One trainer reported to me that he had catalogued his dog's detections at nearly five hundred diverse scents. She could even discriminate specific smells within groups—a lime from a lemon, a lemon from an orange. Amazing.

Chapter 8

"Does His Nose Feel Hot to You?"

Finding a Veterinarian for Your City Dog

I t's a challenge to locate your dog's "dream doctor" in the Big Apple. The sheer number of veterinarians catering to the animals of New York City makes sorting through the D.V.M.s (Doctor of Veterinary Medicine) a daunting task. New York dogs enjoy access to the best canine medicine in the world. Nowhere else are such sophisticated techniques, high-tech equipment, and intensive care so readily available. If a procedure can be done, the chances are that it can be done here. But what if you simply want a cheerful vet to give your dog his shots and clean his teeth regularly, and you don't need all the technology? Not a problem; there are many modest veterinary hospitals with wonderfully talented doctors and staffs to suit your needs. Just know that the big stuff is out there if your dog ever needs it.

Choosing Your Veterinarian

How do you find a veterinarian? With the same amount of care and concern you would take to find your own internist or your child's pediatrician. You can choose a doctor in a larger multiple practitioner veterinary hospital; a solo practitioner; a veterinarian who features house calls as an aspect of his or her service; a veterinarian from one of the shelter clinics whose prices might be a little lower; or a doctor who offers alternative therapies like acupuncture or a holistic approach. Of course, you can simply march your dog in the door at the Animal Medical Center, and consider their entire staff of specialists your private vets. It's up to you, and your dog, naturally.

Whatever the size of the facility, it should meet a few basic standards. First of all, the office should look and smell clean. If you went to see a doctor yourself and the office didn't look orderly, you wouldn't have much confidence in the doctor. Use those same standards on your dog's behalf.

Is the support staff courteous and knowledgeable? Remember, if you need to leave your dog at the veterinarian's overnight or for any period of time, the technicians will probably handle and spend more time with your dog than the doctor himself. While at the veterinarian's, your dog will be under stress. The staff should be able to deal with *whatever* shenanigans your dog may dish out with professionalism and competency.

How big is the support staff? Do a quick head count. You want to feel that there is enough manpower available to handle things even if the phone is ringing, the doctor is calling for assistance, one dog needs a bath, another needs to be observed coming out of anesthesia, *and* an emergency rushes in the door! A practice with a large enough staff will be able to address your dog's needs promptly, no matter how hectic the circumstances!

How flexible are the office hours of the veterinarian you are considering? Do they coincide with the times you are free to take your dog to an appointment? Many practices stay open until 7:30 or 8:00 P.M. one or more nights a week and offer Saturday and Sunday appointments as well.

Does your vet make house calls? A few veterinarians in the city *do* offer this wonderful service, and some organize their entire practice to accommodate home visits.

What emergency services are offered? Aside from the several hospitals that remain open twenty-four hours and a very few emergency clinics that stay open until 1:00 A.M. or are only open at night, most veterinarians' offices *do not* keep a staff person on duty twenty-four hours. Customarily, an after-hours answering service will relay your problem to a vet on call, and he or she will return your call to evaluate the situation. Some doctors also carry beepers. Find out *precisely* what emergency procedures are offered when evaluating a practice, and make sure you are comfortable with them. If you are a person who wants to speak to a doctor *immediately* in an emergency, don't choose a practice that is not equipped to accommodate you.

Once you've evaluated services offered by the practice, you can turn your discerning eye to the veterinarian.

As with any doctor/patient relationship, having a comfortable rapport with your practitioner is of primary importance. Does the veterinarian seriously address your concerns? Does he dismiss your questions, making you feel stupid for asking them? Does he seem approachable and willing to involve you in the process, or does he examine your dog in silence? If you don't feel at ease in the vet's presence, that tension will be transferred directly to your dog. You know how your dog reads your reactions to people. You need to feel relaxed with the vet in order for your dog to be able to relax.

Do dogs, especially *your* dog, like the vet? Of course, dogs usually see the veterinarian only when they're *already* feeling lousy. So don't expect your dog to be overjoyed to see your vet, but he shouldn't take an instant and profound *dislike* to the vet. Does the vet like dogs? Does he handle them with wisdom and gentleness? Be sensitive to your dog's reaction to the veterinarian. After all, your dog is the patient. If he doesn't want a particular person working on him, you should respect that. If you are turned off by a vet's approach, or think it doesn't suit your dog, go elsewhere. Remember, most general practitioners in New York treat everything from dogs and cats to rabbits and ferrets. You might run into a vet who treats dogs as a part of his broad practice but is really a cat person.

How familiar with your dog's specific breed is your prospective veterinarian? Remember, *all* purebred dog breeds have specific problems that are passed on genetically. The more your vet knows about your breed, the better service you and your dog will receive. If you have a Border collie and would rather not ask the doctor outright, "How familiar are you with Border collies?" why not just ask the receptionist how many *other* Border collies are clients. The vet's experience with your breed can really make a difference.

Canine Chocoholics Beware!

Although many of us just can't get enough of the tasty stuff, eating chocolate is extremely dangerous to your dog. Chocolate contains theobromine, which when ingested by dogs in toxic doses causes no end of problems, from vomiting and diarrhea to seizures, coma, and death. The amount of toxicity varies, depending on the size of the dog, so if you catch your five-year-old child feeding a few M&M's to your Great Dane, you are probably all right. However, if you have a toy poodle, the same number of candies is cause for alarm. If you find that your dog has ingested chocolate, call your veterinarian, or the **Animal Poison Control Center** at 800-548-2423, twenty-four hours a day.

It's best simply to keep chocolate away from dogs altogether, despite the drooling and big sad eyes you'll get from your canine chocoholic.

Your Job

Choose the best vet for your dog, and provide that vet with the information he needs *to do* his best for your dog. You must be able to provide your vet with a clear, specific description of your dog's symptoms. What time did you first notice a change in his behavior? Have his stools been normal? Is he restless? The better and more complete your information is, the more the vet can do for your dog.

Despite the wonders of modern veterinary medicine, there are incurable conditions and accidents from which *no* veterinarian can save your dog. You should do everything you can to help your dog, but don't expect miracles or blame the vet if miracles don't happen. You should go for a second opinion or seek a specialist if your vet doesn't satisfy your questions. But understand that medicine can only do so much.

If you decide you do want a second opinion, be honest with your current vet. Don't feel that you're sneaking behind his back. A good vet will respect your wishes and provide you with your dog's medical records so that you can pass them along to the consulting veterinarian.

Of course there are instances in which veterinarians improperly treat animals, misdiagnose conditions, or make stupid mistakes. If you can prove your dog was harmed by the veterinarian's actions, you may register a complaint with the **Office of Professional Credentialing** in Albany, 518-474-3817. This office supervises the licensing of both veterinarians and veterinary technicians in New York State.

Trust your instincts, and remember: NOBODY KNOWS YOUR DOG AS WELL AS YOU DO! If you think that there is something wrong with your dog, trust yourself. Don't take no for an answer and keep knocking on doors until you are satisfied that the problem is resolved.

Now, which doors to knock on . . .

Veterinarians

If you are happy with the veterinarian in your neighborhood, and enjoy a good rapport with him or her, GREAT! But if you are looking for a new vet, I have listed some terrific ones in New York City. In doing so I've isolated some of those who offer special services: emergency services and extended hours, twenty-four-hour nursing care, house calls, lower-cost clinics, and alternative therapies such as homeopathic medicine, acupuncture, or a nutritional approach. All the practices listed are "full facilities," meaning that they offer diagnostic equipment such as X rays

Malpractice, Anyone?

If you find yourself in an adversarial situation with a veterinarian, naturally, you can hire a lawyer and pursue the matter legally. But remember, since dogs are considered property, like a stereo or a television, any harm done to them is viewed as destruction of property. It's as though the vet broke your TV. You won't be able to claim damages for pain and suffering or mental anguish for yourself or your dog, so suing is not very satisfying. Also, you won't be able to recover much more than your dog's monetary value. The lawsuit may cost you much more in lawyer's fees than you can ever hope to get back in a court decision.

and ultrasounds, surgery, dentistry, and nursing care. Almost all of the big "famous" practices are listed here under one category or another, and all are strong bets when looking for a veterinarian in New York City.

There are *many, many* other excellent veterinarians in New York City who are not listed here, only because I tried to bring to the attention of the reader those offering special services. At the same time, I'm sure that there will be those who have had less than perfect experiences with the listed vets. I only mention this to remind you that a relationship with a veterinarian is just that, a relationship, subject to mistakes and hurt feelings. I've attempted to include unique practices with good reputations, but I am not endorsing anyone. Your responsibility as a dog owner is to do your own investigations and find the right vet for your dog.

Late-Night Emergencies

It's the middle of the night and your dog is throwing up; where do you go? These offices remain open, staffed with both veterinarians and technicians, for late-night emergencies.

MANHATTAN

Until 1 A.M., East Side

The Animal Emergency Clinic
Manhattan Veterinary Group Ltd.
240 East 80th Street (between 2nd and 3rd avenues)
212-988-1000

Until 1 A.M., West Side

Riverside Animal Hospital
250 West 100th Street (between Broadway and West End)
212-865-2224

Always Open

Bobst Hospital of the Animal Medical Center
510 East 62nd Street (east of York Avenue)
212-838-8100

BROOKLYN

Night Emergencies

Brooklyn Veterinary Emergency Services
453 Bay Ridge Avenue (69th Street, between 4th and
5th avenues)
718-748-5180

THE BRONX

Night Emergencies

Country Animal Clinic
1574 Central Avenue (corner of Tuckahoe Road)
Yonkers, NY
914-779-5000

QUEENS

Night Emergencies

Veterinary Emergency Group of Queens, P.C.
187-11 Hillside Avenue
Jamaica Estates, Queens
718-454-4141

Twenty-Four Hours

Central Veterinary Hospital
73 West Merrick Road
Valley Stream, NY
718-525-5454

Twenty-Four-Hour Nursing Care

In addition to a veterinarian on call, these distinctive practices
keep a trained technician in the office at night. Of course, most
practices will arrange for a staff person to stay, or check in periodically, if they feel your dog needs observation, but routinely
offering twenty-four-hour nursing makes these practices extraordinary.

MANHATTAN

East Side

The Center for Veterinary Care
236 East 75th Street (between 2nd and 3rd avenues)
212-734-7480

Park East Animal Hospital, Inc.
52 East 64th Street (between Madison and Park avenues)
212-832-8417

West Side

Westside Veterinary Center
220 West 83rd Street (between Amsterdam and Broadway)
212-580-1800

House Calls

Ever tried to hail a cab with a sick Great Dane at your side? The veterinary practices listed here offer the luxury of doctors who make house calls! Of course, you can also always make appointments at these offices, but when considering which vet to choose, you may want to select one who sometimes *can come to you*.

MANHATTAN

Dr. Amy Attas
212-581-PETS

A House Call for Pets
240 West 10th Street
212-989-6651

Columbia Animal Hospital
229 West 101st Street (off Broadway)
212-864-1144

Dr. George Korin, House Call Service
349 East 49th Street
212-838-2569
Affiliated with:
Chelsea Animal Hospital
164 West 21st Street
212-243-3020

St. Marks Veterinary Hospital
384 East 9th Street (between 1st and 2nd avenues)
212-477-2688

ALL BOROUGHS
Mobile Veterinary Unit
Central Hospital
94 Avenue U, Bensonhurst
718-373-0240

BROOKLYN AND QUEENS
The Animal Clinic
9518 Avenue L (near Mill Basin, between 95th and 96th streets), Canarsie
718-444-5151

Park Slope Animal Kind
408 7th Avenue (corner of 13th Street), Brooklyn
718-832-3899

Lower-Cost Clinics

Many not-for-profit animal shelters in New York City include medical clinics or hospitals that offer excellent care at reduced rates. You may choose one of these options for your New York dog.

MANHATTAN
East Side
ASPCA Bergh Memorial Animal Hospital
424 East 92nd Street (near 1st Avenue)
212-876-7700

Bide-A-Wee Veterinary Clinic
410 East 38th Street (east of 1st Avenue)
212-532-5884

The Humane Society
306 East 59th Street (between 1st and 2nd avenues)
212-752-4840

BROOKLYN

ASPCA Clinic
2336 Linden Avenue
718-272-9162

Alternative Therapies

It's the nineties, and by now most of us are aware of the differences between "conventional" and "alternative" therapies. These include homeopathic or nutritional approaches to wellness, acupuncture, and chiropractic. Many veterinarians offering these treatments have a foundation in conventional medicine and mix the two approaches, choosing a protocol that they have found most effective in combating specific maladies. They report startling successes with various canine health disorders, from chronic ailments to conditions generally considered incurable and progressive, like arthritis. Perhaps you feel that your conventional veterinarian has exhausted the regular medical treatments for your dog's symptoms, and you're ready to try something different. Whatever your reason for turning to alternative therapies, there are some excellent veterinarians in the New York City area to guide you.

VETERINARY ACUPUNCTURE

As with human acupuncture, veterinary acupuncture involves the stimulation of various points on the body, causing biochemical and physiological changes. Acupuncture increases circulation, relieves pain by releasing many neurotransmitters, including endorphins, the body's own natural pain killers, and stimulates the body's defense systems. Acupuncture has been used successfully for over 4,000 years on animals as well as humans, and is considered one of the safest therapies when performed by a competent acupuncturist. In dogs, acupuncture is commonly used to treat musculoskeletal problems like hip dysplasia, arthritis, invertebral disk disease, and long-term injuries, as well as skin problems, respiratory problems, and traumatic nerve injuries.

MANHATTAN

Dr. Richard Joseph
Dr. Elaine Caplan (also chiropractic)
The Animal Medical Center
510 East 62nd Street
212-838-8100

Dr. Paul Schwartz
Center for Veterinary Care
236 East 76th Street
212-734-7480

OUT OF TOWN

The Vet at the Barn
Dr. Beverly Cappell-King
811 South Main Street
Chestnut Ridge, NY 10977
914-356-3838

Dr. Alan Schoen
Brook Farm Veterinary Center
Route 22
Patterson, NY 12563
914-878-4833 or 203-354-2287

Dr. Paul Schwartz
Center for Veterinary Care
640 Central Avenue
Scarsdale, NY 10583
914-723-0223

HOMEOPATHY

Homeopathy is a system of medicine that works by stimulating an individual's "healing energies" through carefully matched nontoxic remedies. Prepared from plant, mineral, and animal substances, the entire system of remedies is natural.

If you are interested in learning about homeopathic treatments for your pets, you can get more information from the **American Veterinary Holistic Medical Association,** 2214 Old Emmorton Rd., Bel Air, MD 21015, 410-569-0795. An excellent book to begin with is *Dr. Pitcairn's Complete Guide to Natural Health for Dogs and Cats* by Richard Pitcairn, D.V.M., and Susan Hubble Pitcairn (Rodale Press). It outlines a natural approach to animal husbandry, from pet food recipes to drug-free, holistic treatments for common animal disorders. **Whiskers,** 235 East 9th Street, New York, NY 10003, 800-WHISKERS (944-7537), the wonderful pet supply store and mail-order catalogue, also offers literature on natural animal care and a full line of homeopathic, herb extract, and flower remedies.

Some veterinarians practicing with a homeopathic approach are:

MANHATTAN

East Village Veterinarian
241 Eldridge Street (off Houston Street)
212-674-8640

BROOKLYN

The Animal Clinic
9518 Avenue L (near Mill Basin, between 95th and 96th streets), Canarsie
718-444-5151

OUT OF TOWN

The Vet at the Barn
Dr. Beverly Cappell-King
811 South Main Street
Chestnut Ridge, NY 10977
914-356-3838
Combines acupuncture, homeopathy, herbal therapies, and nutritional remedies.

Dr. Alan Schoen
Brook Farm Veterinary Center
Route 22
Patterson, NY 12563
914-878-4833 or 203-354-2287
Combines homeopathy, acupuncture, chiropractic, nutrition, and Chinese herbal treatments.

NUTRITION!

If you are macrobiotic, read on! By building your dog's immune system through diet, and by using blood analysis to pinpoint which nutrients may be lacking, this approach seeks to find natural ways to combat health problems. Frequently combined with homeopathy and acupuncture, it can be very effective, especially with pets suffering from chronic skin conditions.

OUT OF TOWN

Smith Ridge Veterinary Center
Dr. Goldstein
400 Smithridge Road
South Salem, NY 10590
914-533-6066

The Vet at the Barn
Dr. Beverly Cappell-King
811 South Main Street
Chestnut Ridge, NY 10977
914-356-3838

Getting to the Vet

Now that you have some idea of which veterinarian you want for your dog, how will you get him there? Maybe you have a car or a friend's car at your disposal. Maybe you never have trouble hailing a cab. Many of us have big dogs for whom cabs don't stop. In the travel chapter I list several car services in the city that accept dogs, but for a medical emergency, you might want to try **Bill's Pet Ambulance,** 718-478-3060, or **Pat's Ambulance,** 201-696-4877. The schedules for these services vary, but if you can get them, they're equipped with a stretcher that can accommodate even the biggest Irish wolfhound.

The Hospice Option

There is a Hospice program available to city dogs through **No Standing Anytime,** 414 East 73rd Street, and in Chelsea on 29th Street between 10th and 11th Avenues, 212-472-0694. No Standing will permanently care for infirm dogs whose condition has become too much for their owners to cope with, but who with a little extra care can still enjoy life and give love. The dogs live permanently at either No Standing center, surrounded by many new friends and caring workers, and owners come daily for visits. It's sort of like a doggie convalescent home. These old friends

Dr. Kirschner and Louise. When Louise, a seventeen-year-old corgi-terrier mix, began losing her eyesight from cataracts, her owner brought her to Animal Medical Center ophthalmologist Dr. Susan Kirschner. Following an operation to remove the cataracts, Dr. Kirschner decided to further improve Louise's vision—by fitting her with glasses! The prescription for Louise's corrective lenses was based on the average refraction of a dog's lens. This is the first time a dog has been fitted with glasses at the AMC, and Louise is so comfortable with them that she often falls asleep with her glasses on!

Credit: The Animal Medical Center

give so much love and affection in return, that the staff and owners find the experience very fulfilling.

What's So Special About the AMC?

Manhattan's **Bobst Hospital** at the **Animal Medical Center,** 510 East 62nd Street, New York, NY 10021, 212-838-8100, is not only among the most technologically advanced centers for animal medical care in the world, it is also a premier teaching hospital. Like a Columbia Presbyterian or a Mount Sinai, the Bobst Hospital provides a "class" of about forty veterinary students from the best schools in the nation the opportunity to spend a year as interns. Bringing these best and brightest young minds to the AMC keeps the entire institution moving forward, always finding innovative ways in which to treat animals.

The Animal Medical Center is much more than a state-of-the-art teaching hospital. Its twenty-four-hour emergency medical service is the closest thing to a human emergency room for pets. In addition to their superb emergency services, the AMC runs the Donaldson-Atwood Cancer Clinic in collaboration with Memorial Sloan-Kettering Cancer Center and the Cancer Research Institute. This collaborative effort makes the oncology department's capacity to treat animal cancers unique.

In fact, the professional staff of the AMC specializes in more than fifteen fields, from animal behavior therapy to cardiology, gastroenterology, neurology, and surgery. You may be referred to one of their specialists by your own veterinarian or may choose one of their internists to treat your dog on a regular basis. The AMC is frequently the "last chance" for animals with terminal or hopeless progressive conditions. Often vets will refer their patients there when they have done all that they can, so the AMC takes on the most difficult cases. Because of this you may hear someone say, "Oh, my dog died at the AMC." Unfortunately, terrible diseases and accidents can claim our beloved pets and sometimes there is little that can be done. At least with the technology available at a facility like the AMC, you can improve the odds.

Good luck finding your dream veterinarian in New York City. In researching this chapter, I met some extraordinary professionals who help animals in exceptional ways. I also witnessed animals being served by amazing technologies originally developed for use on humans beings. As usual, we New Yorkers truly have access to the most wonderful resources in the country!

Chapter 9

"Come Fly with Me"

Traveling and Vacationing with Your Dog

E ven the most die-hard "Big Appler" gets out of town for a vacation. I've already discussed the options available for using a pet-sitter or a boarding kennel for your dog when he can't join you on your far-flung jaunts. But what *about* having poochie "come with"?

Wouldn't it be more fun to have your pet hiking *with you* up that mountain pass, or running ahead, chasing seagulls on that beautiful beach? Obviously, there are times when you must travel alone, but it *is* possible to take your dog on more trips and vacations than you might think. Extra planning and preparation are needed, but the rewards are great.

What to Consider

First determine if it is *appropriate* for your dog to accompany you. Does he have the "social skills"? Are there gaps in his obedience training? Does he drag you down the street, or jump up when he meets strangers? Your lower back might need a vacation from the strain of his pulling on the leash. If you're constantly correcting him, it won't be much fun having him along. Wait, address the problems, and include him the next time.

Is your dog getting older and a little frail? Maybe the stress and strain of traveling outweigh the benefits. She'll be much more comfortable on her favorite couch, under the supervision of a pet-sitter, until you get home.

Where are you going on your trip? If it's another city, why bring your dog? She won't be allowed in the museums, can't ride the scenic trolley or visit that quintessentially regional restaurant with you. She'll be underwhelmed. Please, she's a New Yorker, what other city could compare?

Are you going somewhere very hot? Might your dog find himself locked in a rental car with the windows cracked, under the measly shade of a palm tree? Leave him home! When the outside temperature is 85 degrees, the interior of a car parked in the sun can reach 120 degrees in only thirty minutes. A dog's normal body temperature is 101 to 102 degrees, and can be overcome by heat stroke with only a 2-degree rise. Brain damage or death occurs when the dog's body temperature reaches 107 degrees. Such horrible scenarios prompted Florida and Michigan to pass laws prohibiting owners from leaving pets alone in vehicles.

But if you've got a dog with manners like a diplomat, who's spry and rarin' to go, and you're vacationing somewhere fun for dogs, bring him along! Many New York dogs regularly commute to vacations in the Hamptons, the Catskills, the Poconos, upstate, or the Jersey Shore, and are proven travelers. If this is a first trip, you and your dog need a little preparation.

Love Your Crate

A crate is *the* "must have" item for traveling with your dog. As I discussed in chapter two, a crate is a wonderful space where your dog can feel secure and at home. When it comes to traveling, don't leave home without one! It's the only way your dog can fly—even if he is small enough to join you in the passenger section, he'll have to remain inside his little crate. If your dog is bigger than a bread box, he'll have to travel in the baggage area in a suitable airline crate.

Despite your best plans, sometimes you just get stuck for a night and need to find shelter in a non-dog-friendly motel. Having a crate and using it might make the difference when you are trying to talk a recalcitrant hotel manager into bending the rules and letting your pet stay with you.

Car Travel

Before you sign on to a two-week auto tour of the Adirondacks, let's make sure your dog is not subject to CAR SICKNESS!

If your dog turns green at the sight of a cab, you may want to consult your vet for a remedy. Consider introducing travel in the "horseless carriage" gently. Hire a taxi to take you both on a brief tour somewhere in town where the pavement is pretty smooth (no, I'm not being facetious) so the trip is as placid as possible.

Ideally, whenever you travel in a car, you would have space to accommodate your dog's crate, so she could ride securely in there. Inside a crate is absolutely the safest place for a dog to be because of the protection it offers in case of an accident. Crates are also particularly helpful for dogs who become "indisposed," since the motion of the car is reduced.

Recently, "doggie seat belts" and protective harnesses for dogs traveling in the back of open pickup trucks have become commercially available. In the event of a car accident, dogs are thrown about and injured in the same way as people. These restraints (as well as the use of a crate in the car) really do help. Why not buckle the pooch in the way you do the kids? You can purchase these in pet supply stores (I've seen them at Petland Discounts) and through most of the catalogues.

I have to say this just once: NEVER LET YOUR DOG RIDE IN THE BACK OF A PICKUP TRUCK WITHOUT A SAFETY HARNESS. A safety harness, combined with some kind of carpet or mat to keep the dog's paws from burning on the hot metal of the bed, is the *only* responsible way to let your dog ride.

I'm not sure if anyone knows *exactly* why dogs are so crazy about sticking their noses out the windows of speeding cars so that the rushing air pummels their sinuses, but it seems to be some sort of canine cult. I always imagine that they are frantically reading all the smells that wash over them in the wind. Maybe they get some sort of "wind high." Anyway, don't let them do it. Bugs can lodge in their ears, noses, and eyes, and they can be struck by foreign objects—pebbles, sand, et cetera. Also, if they are hanging halfway out of the car gulping air, they are likely to be thrown if you have to stop suddenly. Just keep the windows rolled up high enough so that they can't get themselves in a dangerous position.

Some dogs are simply no fun to ride with. They annoy us by barking at other cars, panting anxiously, and jumping back and forth between seats. Serena's ancestral hunting memories lead her to odd behavior when we're on a two-lane road. She typically rides in the backseat, looking out the front. Occasionally, haunted by dreams of mammoths and bison, she'll fixate on some big vehicle lumbering toward us (usually a semi or a bus). She'll stare at it, transfixed, and as we pass it will leap suddenly at the leviathan as it swooshes by, bumping against the window in a surge of hunt lust. This is not such a terrible problem, but it can catch me off guard. If your dog has annoying car habits, you should speak to your trainer about how best to combat them. They may seem just bothersome and harmless, but a dog who's rambunctious in the car is a *real* hazard. The time and attention it takes you to deal with its distractions are dangerous moments when your eyes are off the road. Use a crate, a dog seat belt, or consult your trainer.

A Safety Notice

Anytime your dog gets in or out of a car, there's a chance that the end of his leash may get slammed in the door as the car pulls away. Impossible, you say? Not! It happens a lot, and is as likely to occur while getting out of a cab as your boyfriend's Range Rover.

A trainer told me a rather scary story. She had arranged to deliver a golden retriever back to her owner, who lived in Tribeca.

To make things easy, they agreed to rendezvous near the Holland Tunnel because the trainer was on her way to an obedience match in New Jersey.

The trainer pulled over to the curb where the owner was waiting and jumped out, leaving the dog sitting in the passenger seat while she unloaded the dog's crate. Then she jumped back in the car as the owner took the dog out of the passenger's door, and pulled away. You guessed it. The end of the leash got slammed in the door as the dog got out. Trying to coordinate the golden's crate, toys, and provisions, the owner didn't realize that her dog wasn't at her side until it was too late. Already a few blocks ahead and intent on merging into the tunnel traffic, the trainer didn't notice the owner waving crazily for her to stop.

Fortunately (for once) the tunnel was backed up, and traffic was bumper to bumper, moving five to ten miles an hour. The trainer noticed oncoming vehicles flashing their lights, but ignored it.

Emerging in New Jersey, the car behind her zoomed up next to her, the driver wildly gesticulating for her to stop. She looked down at the passenger-side door and saw the end of the leash sticking out. Her heart in her mouth, she leaned over and opened the passenger door, afraid to see the dragged body. Miraculously, the golden jumped into the car, panting but uninjured. Having no choice but to follow the car pulling him, that dog had placidly trotted alongside all the way through the Holland Tunnel!

So, please be extra careful whenever your darling pooch gets out of a car!

Up to Connecticut and Out to the Hamptons

It is possible to travel out of town with your dog on public transportation. **Metro North Railroad,** 212-532-4900, serves lower Connecticut, Westchester, Putnam, and Dutchess counties from Grand Central Station and allows "one lap dog per train car." Fortunately, their definition of "lap dog" is *very broad*; well-mannered large dogs—who stay on the floor, not on your lap— are allowed at the discretion of the conductor. Serena and I use Metro North regularly, and we have never had a problem, in fact, it seems as though having a German shepherd when you were little is a prerequisite for becoming a conductor on Metro North.

The **Hamptons Express,** 212-861-6800, accepts dogs with a few stipulations: Small ones must be in carriers and large ones must be muzzled. Dogs can ride on the **Hampton Jitney,** 800-936-0440, but they must be crated, or in a carrier, making it very difficult for large-dog owners.

Air Travel

Up, up, and away is often the necessary mode of transportation for you and your dog, and nearly one thousand animals fly daily within the United States. Of course, you need to be aware of a few things to ensure a safe and stress-free flight for your dog.

Following several gruesome incidents in recent years in which pets died while being shipped, the safety of air travel for animals has been contested in the press. The USDA Animal and Plant Health Inspection Service is in charge of investigating pet deaths on airlines, but they are not required to compile statistics. The *Los Angeles Times* reported (July 28, 1993; also in *Dog Fancy*, June 1993, page 43) that the USDA estimated that in

Dog-Friendly Car Services

If you need to get around town and have trouble hailing a cab with your dog, you might want to become "permanent friends" with a local car service. Having a regular service familiar with you and your dog can literally be a lifesaver in an emergency. I've listed a few services, but the best thing to do is to find one in your neighborhood, go over there with your dog, and introduce yourselves. If they've met you, and feel confident about your dog, you'll get better service. Here are a few who assured me that taking a dog would be no problem:

Apple Express, 718-622-2222
Bennett, 212-927-1500
Car 24, 212-212-2424
Emerald, 718-615-1000 (Brooklyn)
New Concord, 718-731-2222 (the Bronx)

1990, seventy-one animals died in aircraft baggage compartments, mainly from suffocation or heatstroke. These deaths are frequently unreported, and airlines often record pet deaths as lost baggage.

How to Avoid a Bad Air Experience

Traveling during hot weather is the common denominator in most horror stories. If you find yourself stuck on a hot runway, with your dog in baggage, there is little you can do but hope for the best. Returning to the terminal to unload a dog would delay the flight's takeoff. Voice your concerns to a steward, and be sure that the pilot knows there is a dog on board (some airlines have told me that the pilot can alert the tower, and get off the ground sooner, if there is a dog in baggage). By federal aviation guidelines, the airline is not supposed to accept animals in baggage if the temperature is too high.

The only way to avoid this situation is to schedule your flights from hot climates accordingly. Fly very early in the morning, when you could afford to lose an hour or two before the heat hits, or late in the evening when the heat of the sun is gone. Ask what "equipment" or type of airplane is scheduled for your flight. Always try to fly on the largest, newest planes, because they have more space and better air-conditioning systems.

When you purchase your ticket, you will have to tell the airline that you plan to fly with your dog. They will reserve the space in either the baggage compartment or the main cabin if your canine pal is small enough to stay with you in the passenger cabin. There are usually limits as to how many dogs they can accommodate in either space, so make sure the information is in your flight record. If you decide to bring your dog *after* you have purchased your tickets, call the airline immediately to inform them.

What You'll Need

Federal law requires you to carry a current health certificate from your vet attesting to your dog's fitness and vaccinations

For the Small Dogs in the Audience

If you've got a little guy who can ride in the passenger cabin with you, he must remain in his kennel. A great investment for small-dog owners is the **Sherpa Bag,** designed by former flight attendant Gayle Martz. With its hard bottom and soft nylon mesh sides, this airy, unique carry-on accommodates small dogs more comfortably than a standard crate. It even has side pockets for your vet's papers and dog toys! The Sherpa Bag is available at better pet boutiques or directly from **Sherpa's Pet Trading Co.,** 357 East 57th Street, #15A, New York, NY 10022, 212-838-9837. Prices range from $60 to $80.

when you travel between states by air or car. All foreign countries require their own documentation as well as a health certificate filled out, usually no more then ten days before the flight. Other countries have their own import forms, available through the consulate, as well as customs clearance documents. Check with your airline, the capital of the state you are flying to, or call the consulate of the foreign country beforehand so that you have enough time to assemble the necessary paperwork.

To make all this a little easier, the **ASPCA** puts out a booklet entitled "Traveling with your Pet," that lists the many safety concerns you should be aware of, as well as the documentation requirements for over 177 countries. To obtain a copy, send $5 to The ASPCA Transportation Department, 424 East 92nd Street, New York, NY 10128. If you have further questions, call the ASPCA, 212-876-7700, ext. 4402.

Other Problems to Avoid

A chillingly common problem occurs when dogs escape from crates and are lost, or killed, on roads in or around the airport. Be sure that your dog's crate is securely closed and that your dog is wearing a flat collar with an ID tag that includes your name and phone number. NEVER PUT YOUR DOG IN A CRATE WEARING HIS CHOKE-CHAIN TRAINING COLLAR! When he lies against the door or sides, the rings can slip between the wires and become stuck. The dog can panic and choke himself or break his neck.

Mark your crate clearly with **LIVE ANIMAL** in big, bold letters, as well as arrows indicating which way is up (baggage people can get confused), and a sign on the top with your dog's name, home address and phone number, vacation destination address, and most important, FLIGHT ITINERARY. Your dog is much more likely to be loaded *on* flight number 1379 to Albuquerque if there is a big sign on his crate *reminding* the baggage folks to load him.

When I fly with Serena, I don't board the plane until I see the baggage handlers loading her. I lurk by the window, craning my neck until I see her being wheeled out to the plane. If the stewardess tries to urge me on board, I explain that I'm waiting to see my dog loaded and have always found them friendly and understanding.

Again, when booking your flights, think first of your pet's needs. Travel early or late from warm destinations. Fly directly whenever possible, making the trip as short as you can. If you can't avoid a stopover, and need to change planes, make sure that there is enough time between flights for your dog to be unloaded from the first plane, transported to, and loaded on the next leg of the journey. Remember how many times you have landed in terminal B and been told that your connecting flight is leaving in five minutes from terminal E?

While traveling with Serena, if I can't fly directly, I'll choose a connection with a long enough layover that I check her through to the first stop, not our final destination. During our hour and a half layover in Atlanta, I collect my dog, take her outside for "airing," see that she has a drink, and basically make sure that she doesn't spend the hour and a half stuck in her crate suffocating from heat or freezing from cold in some baggage room. When it's time for the second flight, I check her in—to our final stop. Again, I wait to see her boarded before I board, continuing our journey knowing that I've done the best I can to make traveling safe and comfortable for her.

Don't feed your dog within six or seven hours of a flight, but see that he gets a chance for a drink before takeoff. A brilliant trick is to freeze water in a small margarine-type container the night before the flight. When you load your dog at the airport, you can attach the container filled with frozen H_2O to the inside of the crate door with wire or string. As the water thaws, your dog can enjoy refreshing licks throughout the flight. Many crates come with little plastic dishes designed to snap on the wire mesh for just this purpose. I think that this ice dish trick is *the neatest* thing since the Sony Walkman!

If you want to go first class, **Cold Spring Products, Inc.,** Stanfordville, NY 12581, 800-848-8231, has designed a "Canine Transit Kit" especially for travelin' dogs. It's a leakproof self-contained, disposable watering system that snaps easily onto your dog's airline carrier, providing refreshing H_2O during the trip.

Be sure to give him a chance to "go" the last thing before he is loaded into his crate at the airport. This can be one of those "best-laid plans" scenarios. Of course your dog may be too excited at the airport to go, or may not be able to find a spot to his liking.

My girlfriend Susie has had problems with the "airport pit stop" on several occasions. Susie is a very successful opera singer who travels the world to different engagements accompanied by her black miniature poodle, Miss Liberty, or "Libby"— Susie got her on the Fourth of July. Once, flying from L.A. to Paris, they were delayed leaving the west coast, and arrived in New York with barely time to rush to the connecting flight. Libby is small enough to ride with Susie, in a pet carrier under the seat. Since she had already been in the carrier for seven hours, with another seven-hour transatlantic leg ahead, Susie wanted to give her a chance to "do her business." With passengers already

Thinking About Taking Your Pet to Europe? Do It!

Traveling in Europe is a joy for the American dog owner accustomed to the restrictions on dogs in our society. Europeans welcome dogs as integral members of the human community. This basically means that your well-behaved dog may accompany you just about wherever you go: in restaurants, shops, trains, gardens, et cetera. Hotels don't even make a fuss. So why not bring your dog along to enjoy the Swiss Alps or the gardens of Versailles? Just plan ahead, and remember, everyone—humans and canines—gets wiped out by jet lag!

boarding the flight, Susie dashed outside with Libby, and put her down on the pavement. No luck. As precious minutes ticked away, Libby sniffed around agreeably but gave no sign of "getting busy." Libby travels around the world with Susie, and she is trained to use "Wee Wee Pads" in the house and grass outside, but here she was surrounded by pavement. As far as Libby was concerned, there was *not* a suitable spot to relieve herself. At the last possible moment, in a flash of invention born of desperation, Susie ripped the luggage tag off the carrier and put the three by five-inch wrinkled piece of paper on the ground. Libby immediately trotted over, squatted delicately, and used the luggage tag with amazing accuracy. Victory! Susie scooped her up and raced back inside, making the plane just as they were closing the doors.

When You Arrive

When you land at your destination, go directly to the baggage claim area to pick up your dog, and insist that he is promptly delivered to you! The second most dangerous time for traveling animals is when they are unloaded and brought into the terminal. If, during the flight, your pet manages to open his crate, he might jump out and run away in confusion, or be injured when he is being unloaded. A careless worker might misread his tag and put him on the wrong cart to a distant terminal where he might be left to languish in heat or cold. If you are not on hand in baggage claim, he could sit in his crate unsupervised. The best protection you have is to be present at the baggage claim area yourself to inquire after your dog if he is not delivered quickly.

Shipping Your Dog

You might need to send your dog by air when you cannot accompany him or her. Perhaps you go on that vacation to the Florida Keys, decide that Margaritaville is the life for you, call your roommate and tell her to send what she can box and give away the rest, you're staying. What about the dog you left in her care? He'll have to be shipped. Maybe your company has relocated you to their new office in Minnesota and you need to go out there a week in advance, to check out the new condo they've arranged for you, and your dog will be sent later. Or maybe you got a role in your first feature movie, but it shoots for eight weeks in Australia, and you decide to send your dog for a visit to your mom in Washington State while you're away.

When you need to ship your dog, you can either arrange the travel yourself or go through a service. For a fee, the service will not only book the best possible flight for your dog, but will take care of the necessary paperwork, pick your dog up from you, see that it is cared for, acclimated to its kennel, loaded safely on the plane, *and* will arrange pickup and transportation at your dog's destination.

This "travel agency" arranges shipment for pets:

The Animal Travel Agency
1926 Deer Park Avenue
Deer Park, NY 11729
516-667-8924

Operated with the Willow Pet Hotel (the Wald-Arf of pet hotels) by the same family since 1969, now under the enthusiastic care of son Marc Rosenzweig, the Animal Travel Agency can arrange all the details of your pet's itinerary.

Several travel agencies and services cater to pet owners. **Princely Travel,** in midtown, 342 Madison Avenue, New York, NY 10173, 212-286-0506, specializes in luxury trips and will arrange not only your itinerary but your dog's accommodations around the world, as well as groomers, walks, and special cuisines.

The dog-loving gals at **Fresh Pond Travel,** 344 Boston Post Road, Marlborough, MA 07152, 508-624-0400, offer packaged trips for you and your dog. These usually revolve around a seminar or dog show you can participate in, and range from weekends in Martha's Vineyard (around $200 per person) to a full week in Moscow to see (and compete in!) the Russian National Championship Dog Show (about $2,000). Their trips are for serious dog people who can bring their dogs along and compete, as well as for dog enthusiasts. Call them to find out what exciting doggie destinations are up next!

Know where you want to go but aren't sure where to find a dog-friendly hotel? For a $15 fee, **Solveig Foley** at **Pawse Travel Co.,** 170 Goddard Road, Rindge, NH 03461, 603-899-3337, will investigate the area in which you wish to vacation with your dog and will supply you with a list of available accommodations within a 25-mile radius of your destination. A second or third additional area is $12.50, with a long trip usually costing around $40.

A similar service is offered by **DOG GONE,** P.O. Box 651155, Vero Beach, FL 32965, 407-569-8434. If you subscribe to their bimonthly newsletter, which features travel tips and pet-friendly destinations across the U.S., they will also supply you with personalized information and itineraries. A subscriber's first request is free, subsequent requests are $10, and the newsletter itself is a fount of travel knowledge.

The Pet Club of America, Inc., 368 High Street, Athol, NY 12810, 800-223-4747, is a nonprofit organization offering Petfinders, a discount travel club, and a lost pet protection program. With your $20 membership fee (which is tax deductible) you receive a list of hotels accepting pets in your vacation area, a copy of the ASPCA's booklet, "Traveling with your Pet," an advisory on health warnings in the areas you plan to visit, and other bonuses. They will also make many of your travel arrangements free of charge.

Of course, you can make your travel arrangements yourself. More hotels, inns, and motels accept dogs than you might think. The key is finding them. Many of the national chains like Days Inn, Econo Lodge, Comfort Inn, Holiday Inn, and Ramada allow pets at specific locations. It seems to be up to the discretion of the individual motel. By calling the main 1-800 number for the chain and giving them your destination, you can find out if their franchise in the area allows pets.

Aside from hiring a service to plan your trip, the next easiest thing to do is to consult one of the many guidebooks on the market listing hotels and motels, national and worldwide, that accommodate pets. These are available through their publishers or from booksellers in New York (call ahead). Some of the best ones are:

Pets Allowed Directory **($10)**
Modern Systems Computing
9 Green Meadow Drive
North Billerica, MA 01862

Pets R Permitted **($8.95)**
Annenberg Communications
P.O. Box 3930
Torrance, CA 90510

Exotic Port-O-Call? Not exactly. Leslie Day and her dog, Molly, live with their family on a houseboat moored in the Hudson River at the 79th Street Boat Basin. The basin houseboats are populated by many pets, some of which were homeless dogs and cats who found loving homes when they wandered down to the river. Leslie is a teacher and naturalist who founded the 79th Street Boat Basin Flora & Fauna Society, which educates the community about the various plant and animal species living along the Hudson.

Credit: Deb Loven

Vacationing with Your Pet ($14.95)
By Eileen Barish
Pet-Friendly Publications
P.O. Box 8459
Scottsdale, AZ 85252
800-496-2665

Motel 6, 505-891-6161, and **Red Roof Inns,** 800-843-7663, are the two chains I know of which accept pets nationwide. Sure, the towels could be thicker, but you can't beat their prices, and I have always found them friendly and accommodating of my *very big* dog. It is still a good idea to call in advance to confirm since some of the individual members of the chains have weight restrictions on the size of the pet they will allow.

On the opposite end of the budget lodging spectrum are the super-luxury hotels that offer accommodations to pets rivaling those they offer owners. At New York's own **Pierre,** 212-838-8000, canine guests are greeted with a bone-shaped biscuit inscribed with their name, bedded down in wicker baskets with Italian linen mattress covers, and walked by the concierge if necessary. It puts the capital "P" in Posh. Room rates begin at $280 a night and zoom up from there.

Chicago's **Ritz-Carlton,** 312-266-1000, has a grooming salon in the hotel to cater to travel-weary pets. They also offer a gourmet room service menu for dogs—with filet mignon!—welcome pillows, and walks.

On the west coast, L.A.'s super hip **Chateau Marmont,** 213-656-1010, will gladly host your dog, although their approach is a little more relaxed. When I called to check on whether they would walk the dog, I was transferred to the concierge desk, where I posed my question. An amiable (probably out-of-work actor) bellboy said "I dunno, hold on, I'll check." Without putting me on hold, he turned to a coworker, and *actually* said, "Dude, would you walk a dog?" The fully audible response was, "Sure, dude, why not?" Ah, the Golden State.

Is the city driving you nuts? If you and your dog want a weekend away, you need only go upstate or to Connecticut. **River Run,** Main Street, Fleischmanns, NY 12430, 914-254-4884, is a beautifully restored 1887 Victorian home, now run as a superb bed and breakfast in the Catskill Mountains. Located two and a half hours out of the city, River Run offers guests (human and canine) peace and quiet, as well as activities that range from antiquing (there is a country auction every Saturday night in town) and skiing to hiking in the Catskill Forest Preserve. Rates run from $50 to $90 a night. Be sure to mention your dog when you call for information.

The Inn at Chester, 318 West Main Street, Chester CT 06412, 203-526-9541, is a gorgeous spot on twelve acres, with hiking trails, tennis courts, a gym, and a sauna. The freshwater lake a mile away makes for a refreshing swimming vacation for owners and their dogs. Rates range from $105 to $250 a night, with continental breakfast included.

Are you both sick of fighting your way through February snowbanks? **The Lorelei Resort,** 10273 Gulf Boulevard, Treasure Island, FL 33740, 800-354-6364, near St. Petersburg, is "where best friends vacation." A waterfront resort on the Gulf, Lorelei accommodates you and your dog in style. They offer doggie swimming facilities, grooming, an on-call veterinarian, pet portraits, and treats! For you, there is boating, golf, tennis, water sports, and plenty of vacation fun. The Lorelei folks will even pet-sit if you want to take a day and go to Disney World, Epcot, MGM, or exploring. Don't forget the sunscreen, on your dog's nose and inside his ears!

If you decide on a Florida vacation, the big attractions have begun to accommodate dogs! All the Disney parks—the Magic Kingdom, Epcot, and Disney-MGM—have added kennels for day and overnight boarding. This way you can bring your dog with you and know that he/she is well cared for and supervised. Rates are about $6 a day. You can get more information by calling **Walt Disney World,** 407-824-4321. **Universal Studios Florida,** 407-363-8000, provides a kennel adjacent to the main entrance toll plaza, so you can easily leave your dogs, and check in during the day. No overnight stays are allowed. **Sea World of Florida,** 407-363-2613, has added a thirty-five-run kennel this season, with the added plus of the availability of Sea World's veterinarians. Imagine—your dog and Shamu the killer whale could have the same vet!

The ultimate vacation for your dog—as well as for you—is a week at Honey Loring's incomparable **Camp Gone to the Dogs,** Putney, VT 05346, 802-387-5673. For two one-week sessions in June, Honey, her two white standard poodles, and a cast of stars from the world of dog stuff (the best trainers, behaviorists, nutritionists, et cetera, from around the nation) put on a camp that is *the last word* in pet vacation. Held on the scenic campus of The Putney School, about four hours north of New York City, Camp Gone to the Dogs offers a week of instruction, education, and recreation for both of you.

In addition to the daily games (the "Wienie Retrieve," where your dog must fetch a hot dog without eating it, is a CGTTD classic), activities (doggie swimming lessons, dog hair-spinning workshop, doggie softball), and parties (featuring doggie square dancing, and more—Honey is *very* creative), there are daily lectures and classes in topics from "Fixing and Preventing Behavior Problems" and "Introduction to Novice and Open Obedience Work" to "Sled-Dogging for All Dogs." You can take part in any activities you choose, or simply use the week to relax in a beautiful location with your dog. The food is delish (all from *The Silver Palate Cookbook)*, and the all-inclusive price for the week is less than $700 (special services like private obedience lessons with the pros are extra). Just go already! And remember the camp motto: " 'Tails Up!'—If your dog's tail isn't up, we're doing something wrong. Fun is the name of the game."

Armed with the information and tips I've just given you, I expect to see results! Walk into your boss's office next week and announce that you need an extra week of vacation this year—you're going away—with your DOG!

Happy Trails!

Chapter 10

"Hey, I Know My Rights!"

The Law and Your Dog, Canine Health Insurance, and Protecting Your Dog from Loss or Theft

In May 1810, the Common Council of the bustling city of New York created a new city office: the Office of Register and Collector of Dogs. Along with the new office, a law was passed requiring city dog owners to register and license their pets for a sum of three dollars (a *lot* of money one hundred and eighty-five years ago!). Any dog found without a registration tag was to be seized by the city and exterminated. A man named Abner Curtis was hired as the first city dog collector, and he in turn hired dogcatchers, offering them fifty cents for each untagged dog they apprehended.

The law went into effect a month later, in June, but things didn't go as smoothly as the Common Council, or Officer Curtis, had planned. On three separate occasions, when dogcatchers tried to take unlicensed dogs away, angry mobs of more than one hundred New Yorkers quickly formed and stopped the dog's apprehension, freeing the captured dogs and smashing the dog-catchers' carts. This was an expression of popular outrage, and the crowds went unpunished. After several frustrating months during which only a very few dogs were successfully seized without civic unrest, the council and Officer Curtis abandoned their attempt to clear the city of unregistered canines. However, laws governing dogs in New York City did not go away.

So where do canines in our town stand today?

Legal Requirements

Any dog residing permanently in New York City must be vaccinated against rabies and registered with and licensed through the **Department of Health, Veterinary Public Health Services,** 93 Worth Street, New York, NY 11013, 212-566-2456 (Article 7, Section 109 of the New York State Agriculture and Markets Law). By filling out a simple form and paying $8.50, your dog will become a legal resident of the Big Apple. Once you receive the license in the mail, your dog must wear the tag on his collar at all times (New York City Health Code, Article 161, Section 161.04).

As a New Yorker, your dog is subject to a number of other laws. He must be restrained or leashed while outside (New York City Health Code, Article 161, Section 161.05). As much as we complain about having to keep our dogs leashed, it is safer for them. Also, this current law is an improvement over the state of affairs before 1942, when a requirement to muzzle dogs was repealed in favor of the mandatory use of a leash.

No, you can't take the leash off in the park, either. Dogs are prohibited from "roaming at large" in the parks, requiring "a leash no longer than six feet in length" (Section 32 of the Rules and Regulations Affecting Property Under the Jurisdiction of the Commissioner of Parks, Supplement to Rules and Regulations of New York City Agencies, 1946-52). I don't know if anyone has brought up the legality of the expandable "flexi-leashes" we all use, which can stretch up to thirty feet, but this regulation is no joke. It is enforced by park rangers, and a violation is punishable by imprisonment for up to six months, a two-year probation period, or a fine of up to $50. Yipes! Makes you appreciate dog runs, doesn't it?

As I'm sure you know, you must pick up and dispose of your pet's waste, covered under New York City Health Code, Article 161, Section 161.03, which states that "the owner shall not permit the animal to commit a nuisance on a sidewalk, floor, wall, stairway."

But there's more. New York City dogs have all sorts of legal problems, mostly having to do with housing disputes and "dangerous dog" situations.

Housing Problems

The housing outlook is lousy. Many apartment leases prohibit pets. No dogs are allowed in buildings run by the New York City Housing Authority. However, dogs *are* allowed in some elderly housing. You have to look long and hard to find an apartment that will accept your dog, but it's not impossible.

The one bright spot is New York City's Administrative Code, Section 27-2009.1, or the "three month law." This law applies to all rent-regulated apartments and co-ops in buildings with three or more units. According to recent court rulings, it applies to condos as well. Simply put, even when your lease reads "No dogs allowed," if you get a dog and keep her in your apartment without trying to conceal her presence, the landlord, or governing body of the building, has three months in which to formally act against you. They *must* bring a lawsuit. Phone calls, a letter, or even notice to cure don't count, so don't allow yourself to be harassed.

You don't always have to prove that the landlord *himself* knew about the dog. Frequently, courts have ruled that it is enough that a super or doorman was aware of your dog's presence. If the landlord fails to sue within the three-month period, the "no dogs" part of your lease becomes void, and you can legally keep your pet. Even better, any dogs you get after the initial "lease breaker dog" are "grandfathered" in, meaning that you can continue to keep dogs in the apartment. Hooray!

You might have trouble if the landlord claims your pet is a nuisance. A nuisance would be a dog who menaced the neighbors, barked continually, or an owner with many, many pets in one apartment (twenty-six Chihuahuas, for instance). Even so, the burden of proof is on the *landlord* to establish that your pet, or pets, causes a problem in the building. Remember, a "nuisance" is a flexible standard subject to interpretation. Isolated problems, like the time your dog barked for an hour the first day his best playmate, your five-year-old, went off to school, cannot necessarily be considered a nuisance.

The "three month law" was instated not only to help dog owners but also to end a common landlord trick. Frequently, a landlord or super would turn a blind eye to the presence of an illegal dog in the building. But when there was *another* problem with the dog-owning tenant, or they wanted to force the tenant out in order to end the apartment's rent-controlled status, they would suddenly "discover" the dog and push for eviction. Not fair play, but this is New York City real estate we're talking about, and they play hardball.

If your landlord does try to get you out on any of these grounds, remember: You have the right to your day in court! And if your day in court doesn't work out as you had wished, you have the right to appeal!

Dangerous Dogs

Of course we want our dogs to protect us. We live in a city synonymous with crime and danger. If a burglar breaks into my apartment or a fake deliveryman tries to force his way through my door in the middle of the day to rape me, I want my German shepherd to stop him.

But what if she *misjudges* a situation, grabbing the butt of a rude person who bumped into me as he rushed into the subway? How many times have you seen stars after someone hip-checked you on a New York City street? If your dog nips the rude person in your defense, and he or she calls the police and presses the issue, *your dog* could be deemed a "dangerous dog," be seized by the New York City Department of Health, and eventually be put to sleep.

What happens in a New York City dog-bite case depends on the severity of the incident. Typically, the bitee summons the police, who sometimes arrive accompanied by officers from the Department of Health. The dog owner and the bitee tell their stories, and the officers make a judgment on the spot as to whether or not to seize your dog. If it's a severe bite there's not much discussion, and the officers are more likely to use tranquilizers in order to seize him. Several dogs have died at this stage from being over-tranquilized. Your dog is then put in "protective custody," and kept by the city at either the ASPCA, or another facility, until a hearing date can be arranged.

You are supposed to be able to get a hearing within fourteen to thirty days, but sixty to ninety is more likely. The whole time, your dog remains in protective custody. In the meantime, you should certainly consult a lawyer.

Besides wanting to get your dog back, you might be facing a tort liability lawsuit, since the chances are excellent that the victim is scarred physically or mentally in some way. Usually, liability is covered under the blanket home owners' or renters' insurance you may have on your apartment, but most lawyers who have handled these cases say that dog owners should check their policies. Ask your insurance broker directly if your dog is covered under your policy, and if not, add the rider to your policy. Lawyers recommend insurance for between $1 to $3 million in liability.

Courts have generally proven to be relatively "breed prejudiced," meaning that if your dog is an American Staffordshire terrier (one of the breeds falling under the title pit bull) or Dobie, your chances are diminished. If he's a Lab, golden, or small dog, your chances are brighter. Your lawyer will handle things, but you will probably need expert witnesses, animal behaviorists and dog trainers, to testify in defense of your pet. In the best case scenario, the commissioner finds your dog's aggression understandable and warranted, and you are found not liable for any damages. In the next best case, even if you are found liable, you are charged by the court to control your dog better, your home owners' policy absorbs the victim's bills, and you and your dog go your way, older and wiser.

If things don't go so well, the commissioner may determine that your dog is a "dangerous dog" and order you to do any number of things: register him as "dangerous" with the city; muzzle and/or confine him; take out $100,000 of liability insurance; or complete a course of obedience or anti-bite training approved by the commissioner. The commissioner may order the dog removed from the city (your dog gets to live, just not here) or destroyed. This may be accompanied by a liability verdict for more money than your insurance can pay—or you may not have insurance. In addition to losing your dog, you could face severe financial problems.

There is a common belief that "the first bite is a freebie," meaning that if a dog has absolutely no history of unprovoked aggression, the owner should not be held responsible. This is not necessarily true. Liability for dog bites only requires a showing of negligence on the part of the dog owner, or that the owner did not exercise reasonable care. If your dog is off the leash, already a violation of a city code, and bites someone, you are doubly at fault.

If your dog has never shown aggression, and one day, threatened by the funny hat she is wearing, he grabs your aunt's ankle as she comes into your house, well, who knew he was frightened by women in big hats? Even the most conscientious dog owner has no way of knowing if his dog has a "big hat phobia." Since you could not have prevented the incident by reasonable measures, you are not negligent.

But if the next week your dog begins to growl when he sees a woman in a frilly hat and you *do not* stop him from taking a piece out of her calf, you would certainly be found negligent. You could "reasonably" assume that your dog *would* bite her, since he had bitten your aunt a week before. You failed to take reasonable care, and exercise reasonable caution, in supervising your dog.

The moral of the story is: PROTECT YOURSELF AND YOUR DOG! We ask a lot of dogs living in our society: to learn our customs, to communicate with us, and *sometimes* to distinguish between members of our own species. We expect a dog to recognize the difference between a "good person" and an "evil doer," something *we often can't do ourselves*.

Say your bell rings in the middle of the day. If your dog guesses right and bites the would-be rapist, he's a hero. If he guesses wrong, biting the deliveryman, you've got a problem.

This is what I mean by protect your dog:

Don't ask your dog to make distinctions between people. Many dog bites occur on the dog's own property because that's where the dog feels he has sovereign domain. It's his duty to be territorial. Remember, you *want* him to bite the rapist, but if he's aggressive toward strangers, put him in the bathroom when you let the deliveryman in. Don't leave him free on the day the cleaning lady comes. Maybe he loves her, but will she be able to control him if the UPS man arrives? If the high-pitched voices of little children make your dog uncomfortable, don't force him to stay around. Why should all dogs love children?

Just because a parent asks if his toddler can pet your dog, you don't have to say "sure." Remember, the first impulse of little children is usually to grab and pull a big handful of a doggie's skin. If another dog grabbed a piece of your dog's skin, he'd naturally turn around and bite the other dog. You'd better hope your dog doesn't do what comes naturally if it's a toddler pinching him. Most children need to develop to three or four before they learn to pet or stroke a dog's fur. From five to seven they love to "hug" dogs, which is something your dog may also take exception to. Think first of your dog.

If your child has friends over, don't blame your dog if he doesn't understand that children sometimes play roughly. If a playmate pushes your dog's little master down and punches him, your dog might feel that defensive action is warranted. He would see the warning nip on the kid's butt as a gentle persuader to stop beating the living daylights out of his master. The parents of the other kid might not see the situation in the same way. Your dog could lose his life, and unless you're insured up the wazoo, you could have big problems.

Please, just protect your dog from having to make judgments and distinctions he shouldn't have to make. Control his environment. If you have any question about how your dog might react to a situation, put him in his crate, or in another room. DON'T GIVE YOUR DOG THE CHANCE TO BITE SOMEONE. If he does, you both lose.

Anti-Cruelty Laws

There are sections (numbers 353, 355, and 356) within the text of Article 26 of the New York State Agriculture and Markets Law that protect animals from cruelty. It is a misdemeanor, punishable by up to a year in prison, and/or a thousand-dollar fine, to torture, injure, abandon, or starve animals. Although many animal lovers find the penalties much too lenient, they're all we've got right now.

Who to Call

If you encounter *any* legal questions pertaining to your dog you can call the **ASPCA Legal Department,** 424 East 92nd

Anti-Cruelty Laws and You

How do New York's anti-cruelty laws relate to you, a doting dog owner? You should know they exist, because you may need them someday.

A New Yorker sent her beloved dog away for a six-week training course by a so-called expert at the trainer's kennel in the country. At the end of the six weeks, the owner called the kennel to inquire as to when she could pick up her dog. She was told that her dog was very immature and that they would need another week or so to complete his work. A week later, she was told the same story.

When she called about her dog for the third time, she was told to wait another week. Then two days later, the trainer called her to report that her dog had died suddenly. Despite her shock and grief, she had the presence of mind to jump in a car and race up to the kennel to retrieve her dog's body. She took it to a qualified vet for an autopsy. Her pet had been starved to death.

After securing a lawyer, the owner was able to prove the physical condition of her pet before he had entered the "training program," and the tragic manner in which he died. By invoking the Agriculture and Market's cruelty laws, her lawyer was able to get the kennel owner convicted of a misdemeanor. The owner was only reimbursed $500 for her dead dog, which was the maximum penalty at the time, but she and her lawyer eventually prevailed upon the kennel licensing bureau to revoke the trainer's license, hopefully preventing this abuser from mistreating any more dogs.

Street, New York, NY 10128, 212-860-7700, ext. 4550. They are open Monday through Friday, 9:00 A.M. to 5:00 P.M., and will answer your questions, give you information, and refer you, when necessary, to legal representation.

Better yet, just play it safe and call an attorney like **Daryl Vernon**, of **Vernon and Ginsburg**, 261 Madison Avenue, 14th floor, New York, NY 10016, 212-949-7300. Daryl has handled virtually hundreds of cases involving New York dogs and knows more about the legal issues facing our canine friends than I can begin to describe. He is happy to answer questions and concerns over the phone, and can help you head off potential problems with timely action and advice.

Left to right: Anthony LaMontanaro, attorney Daryl Vernon, Jeanette LaMontanaro, paralegal Yoram Silagy, and, of course, Petie the bichon frise. When the condominium they lived in advised the LaMontanaros that Petie had to go, they turned to Counselor Vernon, who took their case to court. In an unprecedented ruling, the second-highest court in New York upheld the LaMontanaros' right to keep Petie. This was the first time the "three month rule" was applied to condominiums. In its ruling, the court said that it would be "pernicious to create an exception." Credit: Petography

Canine Health Insurance

As you probably know from the experiences you've had at the payment desk following a visit to your vet, health care for your dog is not free. If your pet has a serious illness, or accident, a major chunk of change can evaporate—and you certainly don't want to be in the position of denying your dog medical services because of money.

To soften a potential financial blow, several companies offer "pet health insurance." Just like human insurance, there is a membership fee, a choice of deductibles, a maximum amount they will pay per year and per illness, and some perks for joining. Of course, there are limitations. The list of potential health problems excluded from coverage is significant. Exemptions can include: illnesses against which your dog should have been vaccinated; defects believed to be caused by heredity or genetics; or diseases caused by parasites.

However, if your dog is tragically hit by a car, falls victim to cancer, or eats a box of rat poison one weekend in the country and needs prolonged hospitalization, these plans *do* help. The "perks" frequently include membership in a lost pet recovery system, which will help you if your pet is lost or stolen, or insurance against third-party property damage (if your Lab puppy puts a hole in your mother-in-law's best rug, or your Newfie doesn't notice that there is a screen door between him and the swimming pool in your cousin's backyard). Here are two of the health insurance plans available to dog owners:

American Pet Care Association
320 N. Michigan Ave.
Suite 2100
Chicago, IL 60601
(800) 538-PETS

Veterinary Pet Insurance
DVM Insurance Agency
4175 La Palma Avenue, #100
Anaheim, CA 92807
(800) USA-PETS

When Your Dog Is Lost or Stolen

Obviously, the best cure for this is prevention. *DO NOT* let your dog off the leash. *DO NOT* tie him outside a store. *DO NOT* let some "helpful stranger" hold the leash while you check your post office box. Horrible things can happen in an instant.

Networks of pet thieves and dealers who make a tidy profit supplying stolen dogs (and cats) to laboratories have been well documented, most frighteningly in Judith Reitman's 1993 book, *Stolen for Profit: How the Biomedical Industry is Funding a National Pet Theft Conspiracy* (Pharos/St. Martin's Press, available in bookstores or through **In Defense of Animals [IDA]**, 816 West Francisco Boulevard, San Rafael, CA 94901, 415-453-9984). IDA is an organization that monitors, exposes when possible, and raises public consciousness to the problem of pet theft. They have listed central and eastern New York State as one of the *worst* pet-theft areas in the nation, and have reported that 10,000 dogs have disappeared in six months in the Rochester, New York, area alone! Leading breeds consistently missing, with signs that indicated theft, were: Labrador retrievers, golden retrievers, German shepherds, huskies, Dobermans, and other large purebreds. Big dogs are consistently used in "research" in ways that would give you nightmares. Small dogs seem to be stolen in "sporadic waves," when needed by the industry (*Action 81, Inc. Newsletter*, March 11, 1993).

New York City is a favorite target of dog-theft rings because of the concentrated numbers of dogs and their availability. How many dogs have you seen tied to parking meters outside stores or restaurants, waiting for their owners? Each one is a potential victim. Have you ever had a bike stolen? Stealing a dog is a piece of cake compared to breaking a giant padlock and chain. Please take every precaution to protect your dog from theft.

Dogs also just get lost. If the unthinkable happens to your sweetie, there are some things you can do to improve your chances of getting her back. Membership in one of the several organizations and registry services that offer lost/stolen pet protection is a great start. The more you do to make your dog easily identifiable, the better your chances of preventing theft, and getting her back if she gets lost.

Here are a few suggestions if your pet is lost:

Immediately contact the ASPCA and give them a complete description of your dog. Since they are the only shelter accepting dogs on a twenty-four-hour basis, from city dog wardens and the police, this is where he might turn up. Go over there *every day* yourself, or send a friend who would recognize your dog. Let's say you've got a two-year-old Lab-shepherd mix lost in New York City. You may have called "the A," describing your dog as a "Lab mix," but whoever admitted him at the ASPCA took a look at his ear that kind of stands up sometimes and wrote "shepherd cross" on his card. Checking in person is the only sure way to confirm that he's been turned in to the shelter.

Call all the appropriate police precincts with a description of your dog. It can't hurt, and frequently someone will have called the precinct or reported to an officer on patrol that he or she found a dog.

Blanket the city with signs. Keep them simple. Include your dog's description, what kind of collar he had on, when he was lost, and how to contact you. It's best to add a picture of your pet and a reward of $300 or more if possible.

Call **1-800-STOLEN-PET,** the hot line of In Defense of Animals, and **PETFINDERS** at 800-666-5678. These non-profit organizations will counsel non-member as well as member owners who have lost their dogs. Of course it's better to be a member, but they will generously help anyone in distress.

Call **Bob English** at the **U.S. Department of Agriculture,** USDA, APHIS, REAL, 2468-A Riva Road, Suite 302, Annapolis, MD 21401, 410-962-7462. USDA inspectors are the only non-personnel allowed in research labs across the nation. The best thing you can do is send Bob a picture of your pet, but he will take a description of your missing dog over the phone and distribute it to the inspectors so that they will be on the lookout for your dog. The USDA will also send you a list of all the licensed dealers and research labs in the area so you can call and visit them, aggressively looking for your pet.

Stay focused and positive about recovery, and work like mad to find your dog. Your determination and effort may make the difference!

Prevention: Tattoo You

The most popular way to permanently identify a dog is by tattoo—no, not a flowery rendering of a canine with the word *Mother* under it or the motto "Born to Chew" over a bone. An ID/registration number from a dog registry organization is incon-

spicuously and painlessly tattooed on your dog's belly or inner
hind leg. With this lasting means of identification, it is much
easier to locate him or her in a shelter or pound, and it may save
his life if he is stolen for laboratory use.

If thieves have taken your dog, a tattoo is the only thing that
can save him. Laboratories will not accept tattooed dogs from the
dealers the thieves supply. No multinational corporation wants
the publicity of getting caught with somebody's pet dog in their
lab cage. Dog thieves examine pets they've captured and typically release the tattooed ones since they won't be able to sell
them to the dealers. It is important to tattoo your dog on the belly
or inner thigh, not inside his ear. Thieves have been known *to cut*
the tattooed portion of the dog's ear off to prevent identification.

In a broader sense, a tattoo is the only thing that indelibly
links your dog to you. Say your dog disappears and three weeks
later you see a dog who looks exactly like yours living a few
blocks away. You confront the "owner," who claims he got the
dog a month ago from his uncle who lives out of the state. It's
your word against his, and don't think your dog will decide the
matter by his outpouring of love. He may be glad to see you, but
golden retrievers, for instance, are glad to see everybody! Without a tattoo, you have no conclusive way to prove that you are
the rightful owner.

Tattoo registries keep their records permanently, and continue to search actively for your dog. Brooklyn resident Julie
Mosove founded **Tattoo-A-Pet,** 1625 Emmons Avenue, Brooklyn, NY 11235, 800-TATTOOS, in 1972 after seven years of
searching for her toy poodle, Brandy, who disappeared in 1965.
Brandy was never recovered, and Julie realized along the way
that nothing concrete connected her to Brandy. That's when she
got the idea for Tattoo-A-Pet, which is today the world's largest
tattoo registry and boasts a 99 percent recovery rate of its registered animals.

Ninety-nine percent is pretty great, although they don't
guarantee a time limit. Julie told me one of her favorite recovery
stories, about a briard that had been tattooed in San Francisco.
A few months after being tattooed, the dog was stolen and,
despite Tattoo-A-Pet's best efforts, disappeared. Two years later
a briard, found wandering in upstate New York, was captured
and impounded by the local dog warden.

After three months, the dog was put up for adoption, and
was promptly claimed by the young man who had been caring for
the dog while it was in the pound. He was so pleased and proud
of his beautiful new dog that he had made an appointment for

the same afternoon at the dog-grooming shop in town to get his new briard cleaned up. While clipping the matted hair, the groomer found the briard's tattoo, and notified the young man that they would have to check with Tattoo-A-Pet. Within twenty-four hours, the original owner, who had moved from California to Louisiana after her briard was stolen, was driving up I-95 to get her dog back.

When she reached the town in upstate New York and identified her dog, there was yet another wrinkle. The young man didn't want to give up the dog. He had fallen in love with it, and felt that since the dog had been away from his original owner for two years, he had more right to the dog than she did. With Tattoo-A-Pet providing proof that the girl was the rightful owner, he was obligated to surrender the briard.

For a low initial tattoo and registration fee, your dog goes to one of the Tattoo-A-Pet locations, is tattooed on his leg or tummy with a permanent ID number, and is given a tag with the same tattoo/registration number. This provides instant registry, access to the Tattoo-A-Pet twenty-four-hour lost pet hot line, and protection for your pet if he is found. Tattoo-A-Pet guarantees payment of all veterinary and kenneling fees for your pet if he needs emergency medical help. You are still responsible for the fees, but if a vet calls Tattoo-A-Pet in the middle of the night about your dog, who has just been hit by a car, they will assure him that the bills will be paid.

Tattoo-A-Pet is a great service, and it costs only $20 for up to two animals to join. The tattooing process takes less than three minutes and is completely painless. As your mother always said, an ounce of prevention is worth a pound of cure!

The **National Dog Registry,** 800-NDR-DOGS, also registers, tattoos, and recovers missing dogs. They will send you an information packet, complete with a listing of vets who will do tattooing. If your dog is missing, they will counsel you about what steps to take, as well as send a bulletin out to other registries to watch for your dog.

Other Registries

I mentioned **Petfinders, Inc.,** a service of the nonprofit **Pet Club of America, Inc.,** 368 High Street, Athol, NY 12810, 800-223-4747, in the travel chapter as well, since they supply members with itineraries and information about trips. The other wonderful service they offer members is Petfinders. From the moment you report your pet lost, one of their counselors is guiding you as you try to recover your pet. Petfinders also uses a computer bank with your dog's description and medical history, authorizes veterinarians to administer emergency treatment, and guarantees payment for any kenneling that may be necessary until you can be contacted. They also send a description of your dog to every shelter and rescue league within a sixty-mile radius. The Petfinders ID tag your dog wears allows anyone who

The Microchip Mess

You may have heard of the new practice of microchipping dogs for identification. It may be the wave of the future, but we haven't yet worked out all the wrinkles. Microchip identification involves a veterinarian implanting a transponder microchip, about the size of a grain of rice, underneath the skin on your dog's shoulder blades. The chip is programmed with a code number, and gives off a signal at a specific radio frequency. When scanned with a compatible scanner, all the information identifying your pet pops up on a computer screen. Great, right? Aside from the fact that the chips sometimes aren't implanted properly and "migrate" inside your dog, there's an overwhelming problem. There are several companies selling chips and scanners, and they are not yet compatible. So if your dog finds his way to a shelter with a scanner from company A, and the chip you implanted in your dog is from company B, your dog is out of luck. Also, since the chip is not visible the way a tattoo is, it's ineffectual as a deterrent in protecting your dog from theft.

If you're interested, you can get more information from:

IdentIchip, Dept. DF, 72 Overlook Drive, Danville, PA 17821, 717-275-3166

InfoPet, Dept. DF, 517 W. Travers Trail, Burnsville, MN 55337, 612-890-2080

AVID, Dept. DF, 3179 Hamner Avenue, Suite 5, Norco, CA 91760, 714-371-7505

might find her to contact their hot line, and get her back to you ASAP.

Dog ownership is no longer as simple as it may have been when a pup followed you home from school one day and your mom let you keep him as long as he stayed on the porch. In the five boroughs we have thousands, even millions, of dogs living in close proximity to each other and the general public. Please, do everything you can to be a model dog owner.

Be responsible for your pet. Obey the laws governing dogs: register, leash, and pick up after him! Protect your dog by tattooing him and not leaving him alone where he might be stolen or lost. Be considerate of your dog's "comfort level" by not putting him in social situations that overwhelm him and cause him to act aggressively. He's your dog, he loves you and will trust and protect you his whole life. Make sure that you are worthy of all that affection by protecting him as well.

Chapter 11

When That Time Comes

Dealing with Your Dog's Passing

At one time or another, we will all be faced with the deaths of our beloved dogs. Had we anticipated this sadness at the outset, we might never have let the squirmy bundle of puppy, or the lonely older dog, share our life. But we did, and now, here we are.

Is there a way to make this process less painful? Yes and no. You can't numb yourself to the grief, but you can prepare for it by apprising yourself of the options and arrangements you may want to make, and seeking help during your own grieving process.

Another issue too frequently overlooked is what will happen to your pet if *you* precede him. As a concerned, responsible dog owner, you need to consider this question and make arrangements, if necessary, so that he will be cared for as you would want him to be.

What Usually Happens

Depending on the circumstances, your pet could be taken from you abruptly—hit by a car, or stricken by a sudden unforeseen malady, like bloat—or you may be asked to nurse him through the many painful months of a prolonged illness. If your dog's sickness is too much for you to cope with, but he could survive for a few months, or years with some extra care, there is a hospice option available through No Standing Anytime, 212-272-0694. Call for more information. Ultimately, your veterinarian may ask you to make the final decision. It is your responsibility to seek out the emotional support and help that you may need to get through this difficult time.

Many owners choose to walk away, focusing on happy memories of their dogs, allowing the vets to take care of the bodies. But as the tombs of the ancient Egyptians and the Vikings tell us, for thousands of years people have honored the deaths of their pets in ritual fashions. When your pet has passed away, you have several options. You might want to have his remains cremated or you may elect to have a formal funeral and burial at one of the animal cemeteries in the metropolitan area. The important thing is to do what feels right to you.

Cremation

If you choose to have your pet cremated, the ashes can either be placed in an urn or buried in a small plot at a cemetery. Your veterinarian will be able to arrange this.

If you want to make the arrangements yourself, **Hartsdale Cemetery Cremation Service,** 75 North Central Park Avenue, Hartsdale, NY 10530, 914-949-2583, and **Aldstate Pet Cremation Service, Inc.,** 306 83rd Street, Brooklyn, NY 11209, 718-748-2104, will pick up your pet's body from your home, or your veterinarian's office, and return an urn to you. Prices depend on the weight of your dog, and you can supply your own urn or purchase one from them. Their wood urns have a glass front into which you can slip a photo of your dog.

Pleasant Plains Pet Crematory, 75 Stirling Road, Warren, NJ 07059, 800-972-3118, will also pick up your pet and, as they so eloquently put it in their brochure, will "return your pet's body to its original elements." The remains will be returned to you either in a metal box or a permanent urn that you may purchase. They also have a variety of urns available—beautiful pedestals and boxes, as well as urns with picture frames on the front. Since it is affiliated with the beautiful **Abbey Glen Pet Memorial Park,** Pleasant Plains can also arrange for interment if you choose.

You can buy an urn directly from **Glassman Pet Casket & Urn Co.,** 41-45 Astoria Boulevard, Long Island City, NY 11105, 718-274-5703; **The Vase Place,** 65 Webb Circle, Reno, NV 98506, 800-682-VASE; or **Childress Co.,** P.O. Box 35, Afton, VA 22920, 703-949-0527.

If you want a special eternal resting place for your pet far from the winter chill and city grime of New York, **The Gulfstream Pet Cemetery of the Seas,** Box 1157, Jupiter, FL 33468, will scatter his ashes in the warm, tropical Gulf stream.

Caskets

There are caskets as elaborate as you can imagine available for your dog. A pet cemetery or memorial park can sell you one as part of the entire burial package, or you can buy one from **Childress Co.,** P.O. Box 35, Afton, VA 22920, 703-949-0527; or **Glassman Pet Casket & Urn Co.,** 41-45 Astoria Boulevard, Long Island City, NY 11105, 718-274-5703.

Grave Markers

You can choose almost any kind of marker you wish to be placed by your dog's grave. My personal favorite is the "photo engravature" done by **Stone Imagery,** P.O. Box 2645, Carlsbad, CA 92018, 619-434-4493. Any black and white photo and personal message can be turned into a stunning engraving on polished black granite, 12 x 12 x 3/8 inches deep. The detail in the photo is remarkable, and it is very moving to see your dog's image on such beautiful stone. The engravatures are very reasonably priced, ranging from $125 to $200.

Other companies specializing in pet memorials are **My Pet**

Granite Memorials, P.O. Box 160, Carlton, GA 30627, 800-524-3054, and **Everlasting Stone,** P.O. Box 995-CF, Barre, VT 05641, 802-454-1050.

Regular monument companies can also supply you with the grave marker you desire.

Cemeteries and Memorial Parks

There are several beautiful cemeteries and memorial parks in the New York City area. Each will collect your pet's remains at either the veterinarian's or your home, and will make arrangements for burial. All will accommodate any type of service you wish to hold for your pet. These can be as simple as a few quiet moments alone in the viewing room with your pet before burial to bringing friends, family, and even clergy to a memorial or funeral service. The staff has seen it *all*, so don't feel for a moment that your wishes are "silly." It is fitting, if you so choose, to hold a service during which you and your closest friends remember the joy your pet brought to you. You can read a poem, play a piece of music which is meaningful to you, or ask the leader of your church or synagogue to say a few words. I can't guarantee that they will comply, but it doesn't hurt to ask. The cemetery frequently is able to refer you to a spiritual leader who can assist you.

Following a viewing or service, the memorial parks usually encourage owners to accompany the casket or urn to the spot of burial, and even to take part in the interment. Of course this is optional, but it can be helpful for you to actually *see* the interment.

You will be able to visit your pet in these beautiful places whenever you wish, and you may find solace in talking to the other pet owners you meet on your visits. The **Hartsdale Canine Cemetery** reports an average of more than five hundred visitors every week, with Christmas and Memorial Day being especially popular (*The New York Times*, January 5, 1986).

These are some of the best cemeteries and memorial parks in the metropolitan area:

A serene fifty-two-acre preserve with picnic areas, a duck pond, and a rose garden, **Abbington Hill Pet Animal Cemetery and Crematory,** 148 Youngblood Road, Montgomery, NY 12549, 914-361-2200, is a lovely spot for your dog. They also offer some unique options. Abbington Hill allows *owners to be buried alongside their pets*, although currently this is only possible with human cremated remains. Considering the needs of the other pets in a multi-dog family, Abbington Hill encourages owners to bring them for a special viewing of the body. This gives the survivors a chance to recognize that their friend is gone, and gives them a sense of closure. Abbington Hill has plots as well as granite mausoleums for the interment of pet animals.

The Hartsdale Canine Cemetery, 75 North Central Park Avenue, Hartsdale, NY 10530, 914-949-2583, is the oldest and most respected pet burial ground in the country. Today over 50,000 pets are buried there, including the pets of such celebrities as Gene Krupa and Kate Smith. The grounds are gorgeous and are well-known for the thousands of flowers that cover the grounds. In the spring, more than 3,000 chrysanthemums are in bloom, in the summer, 20,000 begonias, and wreaths of balsam and spruce decorate the property in December. Hartsdale's sensitive and compassionate staff will guide you through the arrangements and are wonderfully supportive.

Bide-A-Wee Memorial Park, 118 Old Country Road, Westhampton, NY 11977, 516-325-0219, is operated by the nonprofit Bide-A-Wee Home Association. The association also runs a park in Wantagh, New York, which is filled to capacity. Both feature the same caring staff and high principles that have guided the Bide-A-Wee Shelter since 1903. Their services are *very* reasonably priced, although the bill can climb if you add expensive caskets and memorial stones.

Abbey Glen Pet Memorial Park, Route 94S, RD 2, Box 512, Lafayette, NJ 07848, 800-972-3118 or 201-579-9574, is located on eighty-five rolling acres in northern New Jersey, about an hour and a half from New York City. No high memorial stones are allowed at Abbey Glen; it looks more like a wooded park than a cemetery. At Abbey Glen you have several options for burial. The "Hillside Burial" section of the park features a statue of St. Francis of Assisi. The "Woodland Rest" section offers concrete lawn crypts nestled into a wooded cliff side. In the "Country Burial" section, your pet's name is added to the "Gift of Love Memorial," and he is buried, without a marker, in a particularly beautiful zone (this is their most economical option). They also have a special interment section for animals like Seeing Eye, therapy, and police dogs who devoted their lives to public service.

The Regency Forest Pet Memorial Cemetery, 760 Middle Country Road, Middle Island, New York, 11953, 516-345-0600, is another lovely final resting place for pets. You can purchase plots in several ways, from "Tranquil Forest," where a plot will accommodate three interments to "Sleepy Meadow" for the single-pet owner. Their chapel makes a wonderful spot for the service you may want to hold in your pet's honor. Removal and transportation from your home, or the vet's, to their facility is provided as well.

What About the Pets Left Behind?

If you live in a multiple-animal household, then the death of your dog will also affect the other pets. Whether or not the other pet is another dog, or a cat or a bird, the loss of one member will throw the balance off. You must anticipate and accommodate the grieving of these other creatures. Animals mourn.

Elizabeth Marshall Thomas, author of *The Hidden Life of Dogs*, spoke at a Learning Annex event last year. A woman asked her if dogs feel grief. "Of course they do," she said simply and elegantly. "Grief and a sense of loss is the price paid by creatures who have the capacity to bond."

Try to spend extra time with the surviving pets. It's safe to assume that they are missing the one who's gone and may be particularly needy. They also may feel anxiety as well as grief. If they haven't had a chance to see the body and sense the presence of death, all they know is that one of their pack has disappeared. What might happen to them? Be aware of these issues, and consult a behaviorist if they develop problems like destructive or self-mutilative behavior. You can expect them to be gloomy and depressed, but keep a close eye on the situation.

If you want guidance during this difficult time, call **Animal Behavior Consultants, Inc., Dr. Peter Borchelt, Dr. Linda Goodloe, and Valeda Slade, M.S.** at their low-cost help line, 212-721-1231. They make house calls and treat dogs, cats, and other animals.

What About You and Your Family's Emotions?

Losing a pet can be every bit as upsetting and depressing as losing any other beloved family member. Whether you live alone with your dog, or have the added challenge of having to explain the loss to a child, it is a particularly difficult process. Fortunately, wonderful help is available from pet loss grief therapists who specialize in helping clients work through their emotions during and after the loss of a pet.

Charlene Douglas of **Washington State University's People-Pet Partnership Program,** 509-335-1303, or on the Internet, DouglasC@wsuvm1.csc.wsu.edu, reports that nearly 80 percent of the people who contact her are grappling with a euthanasia decision. Grieving pet owners also have to face unsympathetic people. "As a society we're unprepared to talk about death; as a result, people sometimes say silly or dismissive things to cover their own discomfort," Charlene says. When your grandmother dies, everyone knows the appropriate response is "I'm sorry, you must feel awful," but when your pet dies, people are just as likely to say "Pull yourself together, it's only a dog."

"Pet owners in grief need to hear that they're not crazy," Charlene says. "It's reassuring and comforting to talk to someone who cares."

If you're considering getting another dog, it's important to work through any feelings you might have of betraying your old pet. You must fully understand that a new pet brings a new relationship. Don't get a new dog if you secretly want him to be your old dog all over again. You are putting unfair expectations on him, and limiting your own scope of enjoyment. The new pet is likely to bring new and different pleasures, and problems, to your life.

Several universities sponsor pet loss support help lines, staffed by counselors trained in grief therapy. The counselors are frequently either veterinarians or vet students, so they often understand the medical issue you may need to discuss. All the hot lines accept messages twenty-four hours a day and return your call the same evening. They will send you written materials, and will give book references on request as well.

Pet Loss Support Helpline, 708-603-3994, sponsored by the Chicago Veterinary Medical Association in conjunction with the Delta Society

Pet Loss Support Hotline, 916-752-4200, Center for Animals in Society, University of California at Davis

Pet Loss Support Hotline, 904-392-4700, ext. 4080, University of Florida at Gainesville College of Veterinary Medicine

Pet Loss Support Hotline, 517-336-2696, University of Michigan College of Veterinary Medicine

Again, you can always call **Charlene Douglas** of **Washington State University's People-Pet Partnership Program,** 509-335-1303, or on the Internet, DouglasC@wsuvml.csc.wsu.edu. Charlene actually answers the phone, weekdays during business hours, and will return calls left after-hours. She is a pleasure to talk to, and will send you a giant package full of informative articles, poems, and stories appropriate for adults as well as children.

Grief Therapists in New York

New Yorkers have one of the very best pet loss programs right here in our own backyard. In 1981 the **Animal Medical Center,** 510 East 62nd Street, New York, NY 10021, 212-838-8100, established the Institute for Human/Companion Animal Bond, to study and foster relationships between people and pets. At the same time, the Department of Counseling was established. Certified social worker and grief therapist Susan Cohen runs the department, counseling grieving pet owners and helping them with euthanasia or treatment decisions.

The Department of Counseling offers their services free of charge to anyone, not just clients of the AMC, who is suffering through a pet's illness or death. Phone consultations are offered, as are in-person sessions and a regular support group. The support group meets every other Saturday afternoon at the AMC.

Dr. Carole E. Fudin, 145 East 15th Street, Suite 1F, New York, NY 10003, 212-473-0932, has a private practice in general psychotherapy, with specialties in pet loss, euthanasia decision-making and the psychology of medical veterinary practice. She sees individuals, families, and groups. Because of her interest in the tensions and stresses surrounding the practice of veterinary medicine, many of her clients are veterinarians themselves.

The **Bide-A-Wee Home Association,** 410 East 38th Street, New York, NY 10016, 212-532-6395, offers individual and group bereavement counseling at both the Manhattan shelter location and the **Wantagh** shelter, 516-785-4199.

Who Will Take Care of Your Dog If You Go First?

Most of us do not want to think about this scenario, but we probably should. If you are lucky enough to have a partner, friend, or family member who will keep your dog if you die (or if you need to be hospitalized), then you have nothing to worry about. If you are not so sure, you might want to make some arrangements ahead of time. Don't trust to the fact that everything will magically be taken care of, or that if your dog is put up for adoption he/she will find a happy new home. Remember that most of the "no-kill" animal shelters in the metropolitan area have a long waiting list. If your dog is dropped off without previous arrangements, he may not be admitted and may end up in a city pound with only a few days to be adopted before he is euthanized.

If you have friends or family who have agreed to look after your pets, the safest thing to do is to make it legal. **The Committee on Legal Issues Pertaining to Animals** of the Association of the Bar of the City of New York has put together an informative booklet entitled "Providing for Your Pets in the Event of

Helpful Books

There are many great books on the market about pet loss and grief. Three of them are:

Coping with Sorrow, by Moira Anderson, M.Ed., Peregrine Press, 1994.

When Your Pet Dies: How to Cope with Your Feelings, by Jamie Quackenbush and Denise Graveline, Simon & Schuster, 1985.

The Loss of a Pet, by Wallace Sife, Howell Book House, 1993.

Your Death or Hospitalization." You can obtain a copy by calling the association's Office of Communications at 212-382-6695.

Alpha Affiliates, 103 Washington Street, Suite 362, Morristown, NJ 07960, 201-539-2770, a nonprofit organization that studies and fosters the relationship between people and animals, will provide you with durable power of attorney for pet care. The document offers guidance and the means to authorize care for your pet should you be unable to do so. You will be asked to name a specific agent, as well as a backup, who will be responsible for your pets. You will also need to make financial provisions for your pet's continuing care in your estate. You can use Alpha Affiliates' document itself, or it can serve as a model for a section you may want added to your will.

The Humane Society of New York, 306 East 59th Street, New York, NY 10022, 212-688-4761, offers a **Surviving Pet Care Program**. Although due to space limitations it is open only to small dogs, when your pet is enrolled in the program, the society will assume custody of him when you are gone, care for him, and find him a permanent new home. There is no minimum charge to join, but since the society is supported by contributions, acceptance into such a program *should certainly* be followed by a bequest if at all possible. To prepare, have your attorney clearly specify in your will that you wish your animals to be given to the society. Because wills are sometimes not read until a few weeks after death, the society suggests that you restate the information in a letter of intent, and leave it with a friend or relative who can call the society immediately so that your dog doesn't languish, alone and uncared for, in your apartment. Including up-to-date medical records and information on your pet's temperament and preferences will ensure that he gets the best continuing care.

The Bide-A-Wee Home Association

One of New York's best shelters, the Bide-A-Wee Home Association, will immediately accept your dog or dogs into its program when accompanied by a charitable bequest in your will. There is no minimum amount suggested, but as generous a donation as possible is recommended. Remember, you can leave a percentage of your estate, a specific dollar amount or piece of property, or you can simply name the charity as a financial beneficiary, meaning that they receive whatever remains after your heirs take their share. Your attorney must include a notation in your will that stipulates your intentions to give to Bide-A-Wee, and that your pets should go there. Be as specific as possible about your dog's needs and any special medical or temperament problems he might have. Be sure to arrange how and when your pets will be transported to Bide-A-Wee. They will be happy to guide you through the entire process. Call the **Bide-A-Wee Home Association,** 410 East 38th Street, New York, NY 10016, 212-532-6395, and ask for the **Development Office.**

Remember, give yourself the time to sort through your emotions. An acquaintance of mine has just passed through the painful loss of her dog, and I want to tell her story, not because it

Memorial Donations

Even after your pet is gone, why not let his memory help other animals by making a contribution in honor of your dog to one of the very deserving shelters, rescue groups, guide or service dog schools, animal hospitals, or organizations helping animals. You probably have a favorite already, but if not, here are a few:

The ASPCA, 424 East 92nd Street, New York, NY 10128, 212-876-7700

The Humane Society of New York, 306 East 59th Street, New York, NY 10022, 212-688-4761

The Bide-A-Wee Home Association, 410 East 38th Street, New York, NY 10016, 212-532-6395

Animal Rescue Network of East Harlem, 511 East 118th Street, New York, NY 10035, 212-860-7746

The Animal Medical Center, 510 East 62nd Street, New York, NY 10021, 212-832-5634

Pet Owners With AIDS/ARC Resource Service (POWARS), Inc., P.O. Box 1116, Madison Square Station, New York, NY 10159, 212-744-0842

has a happy ending but because it includes so many of the feelings that accompany our dogs' passing away.

For fifteen years the distinguished silver gentleman, Herr
Otto of Blue Snow, shared Susan's life. From a line of champion
miniature schnauzers, Otto had never set foot in the showring
but had the style and grace of his famous relatives. He was simply Susan's champion. After a long day at work, she knew he
would be there to gaily greet her when she got home. He always
ran from the front door to jump up on her bed, making himself
taller, offering a paw in a formal handshake of welcome. When
Susan and Otto went away on weekends to their house by the
shore that he so dearly loved, he would throw himself down on
the grass, rolling over and over joyously, happy to be back in the
country. Always ready to join in her adventures, Otto was
equally content to nuzzle his head under her arm as Susan sat
reading on the sofa, to fall asleep with his head on her lap. He
knew her triumphs and her sorrows. He was her dearest and best
companion. He was her heart.

In early June of his fourteenth year, Susan noticed the bump
on Otto's front leg. They were at the shore for the summer, and
when Otto went to have his teeth cleaned at their favorite vet on
the island, the growth was removed. The biopsy brought bad
news, a malignant melanoma.

Otto seemed fine, and the incision quickly healed. As
spunky as ever, Otto was blissfully unaware of the cloud that had
settled over their lives. Not so Susan. She had discussed the
options with her vet and had considered the weeks of confinement and painful procedures an aggressive therapy would mean.
She knew the prognosis. Because of his age, they would take a
noninvasive approach. She brought her dog home.

A month later there were more lumps. At a visit to the vet in
September, Susan was told that Otto might only live two more
months. Still, he seemed fine. He played and romped as usual.
Back in the city, he sniffed the crisp air off the river, sifting
through the smells to find the tinge of salt in the air, looking for
a trace of their beach home. They went out to the island on
weekends even later than usual that year. The trips gave Otto so
much pleasure, and there was something about the happy way he
rolled in the grass and accompanied her on their long walks that
made Susan think that there *must* have been some mistake, that
their life together could never end.

Still he continued to fight the odds. The holidays came and
went, and the full force of a northeastern winter held New York

in its icy grip. Otto fought the elements, climbing over snow-banks and through slush on the streets, just to reach the park. He was holding his own so well that Susan really *did* begin to dare to hope that the vet had been wrong. But in February Otto's strength began to fail. By the middle of the month, he was barely eating. One Friday when Susan came home from work, there was no Otto at the door. She found him too weak to even lift his head, his stub of a tail moving silently in greeting, apologizing to her for not offering a proper welcome.

The next morning he was still too weak to walk. With dread, Susan bundled Otto into the car. If it was to be, she wouldn't let it end this way. She would get him back out to the place he loved best, to smell the salt air, not the city grime. They drove directly out to the vet, where Otto was examined.

The kindly vet established that Otto was not in pain but was in the final phase, the cancer having gone into his central nervous system. He counseled Susan to take the dog to their house and watch him for forty-eight hours. As long as Otto was not in pain, there was no reason to end it so abruptly. Susan needed the time with him, even if it was to be a brief reprieve.

Once more she took her sweet Otto to their beloved house. She tried to make him as comfortable as possible by doing everything they had always done, cooking his favorite meal, lifting him to lie in his favorite spots. At some point she realized that it was hopeless to try to recreate every pleasant memory. It hadn't been *what* they had done together, but that they *were* together.

Sunday morning, Otto was disoriented. It was February 20. Susan knew that it was time to say good-bye. She called the dear vet, who met her at his office. They talked everything over, and finally, holding Otto in her arms, Susan felt him relax, his darling silvery head drooping heavily on her shoulder. It was done. A long, gray, cold ride back to the city awaited her, and an empty apartment.

The next few weeks were a blur, not only because her eyes were so often filled with tears, but because she felt numb. She received Otto's ashes in a beautiful brass urn, friends expressed their sadness, time passed. She felt dead inside. The loss of this little dog had turned her world upside down. She had been fine before there ever was an Otto. Why had she opened herself up to this much pain by loving him so?

A month later two things happened. Susan received an acknowledgment letter from the Cornell Veterinary School letting her know that her vet had made a contribution toward research against canine diseases in Otto's name, and Otto's groomer on the island called to see how Susan was doing. The vet's gift touched Susan, making her feel that something positive had come out of all the pain of losing Otto. The groomer's call raised another issue. After some small talk, she asked Susan if she was thinking of getting another dog. "Oh, Aileen," Susan said, "I just don't know if I'll ever be ready for that again." The groomer said she had heard of a wonderful litter of miniature schnauzers born to a breeder on the island. "I'll just give you her number, " Aileen said. "Maybe someday you'll need it."

For another month the scrap of paper with the breeder's phone number sat, goading Susan. She missed *Otto*, she didn't want a different dog. She absolutely didn't *ever* want more of this pain. If she got another dog, wasn't she just starting down the same road again? But then . . . despite her busy career, family, and friends, she just missed that special rapport, the unique companionship her dog had offered.

Finally, just to get general information, Susan called the breeder. Yes, there were puppies, three males, but she had puppies several times a year, yes, all champion lines, in fact in the past she had exchanged blood stock with the breeder Susan had gotten Otto from, yes, if Susan was interested she could come by.

Another few weeks passed. Early in May Susan was going out to the island for a weekend, and just out of curiosity, she stopped at the breeder's. She hadn't even decided she wanted another dog. Was she betraying Otto? Well, he couldn't blame her for just *looking*.

After a pleasant conversation with the breeder, a laundry basket was brought out. Inside, on a blue towel, sat three tiny Ottos! Three stubby whiskered faces with sparkling eyes looked up curiously at her. She picked one up and felt his little heart beating as quickly and softly as a bird's. Her mind was a blank, but she heard a voice she recognized as her own say, "I'm still not sure, but can I put a deposit on one?" "Which one?" asked the breeder. The puppies had been put back in the basket, but one had immediately scaled the sides and was back at Susan's feet waiting to be picked up again. He had an extra spot of white between his nose and his mouth. "This one," said Susan.

It was crazy. She hadn't even decided she wanted another dog, and here she was putting down a deposit. The breeder assured her that when it was time for the puppies to be sold she usually had a waiting list. Susan was under no obligation, the deposit would just hold Little White Spot for her until she was sure.

Another few weeks of grappling with loneliness and guilt passed. Finally, on Memorial Day weekend Susan was out at the beach house. The weather was gorgeous, just the sort of day she and Otto would have filled with playing, shopping, walking, and snuggling. Her eyes filled once more with tears. She had been mourning Otto for a year since his cancer was diagnosed and she had been given the prognosis. Then she thought, "Am I going to spend another year grieving?"

She called the breeder to say that she would pick up her puppy in two weeks, when she came out for the summer.

Little White Spot had been bathed and groomed to go to his new home. When he strutted out, handsome and adorable, Susan's heart melted. The breeder had all the paperwork ready, his vaccination schedule, his pedigree and registration forms. As Susan scanned the papers, her new puppy in her arms, she gasped in disbelief, and tears suddenly welled up in her eyes. The puppy's birth date was February 20, the day Otto had died! On that lonely, awful drive back to the city after Otto had been put to sleep, Susan had driven past the kennel. At the same time her puppy was being born! And the pedigree! Among the names of the puppy's ancestors were Otto's relatives!

In a daze Susan took Little White Spot out to the car and drove to her vet for her puppy's first checkup.

The whole staff of the veterinary hospital turned out for the arrival of Susan and her new puppy. As they walked in to applause, the kindly vet said teasingly, "What took you so long?" Susan blushed, knowing he meant, "We all knew you wanted another dog, why didn't you know yourself?"

"His name is Andy," she said proudly.

"Well," the vet pronounced, looking down at the sporty puppy standing by his mistress, "Andy is a dandy!"

Susan and Andy out for a stroll.

Credit: Petography

Chapter 12

New York's a Wonderful Town for Dogs and the People Who Love Them

What does New York offer its canine citizens? Personal walkers, shopping, play groups, the best veterinarians—basically whatever their hearts desire. But there are other events, services, and just plain fun that don't fit easily into any of the previous chapters and are of great importance and interest to dog folks.

For instance, where do you go on Christmas Eve for a blessing of the animals service? How do you get your dog started in show biz? When are the big dog-friendly fund-raising walkathons? Who will bark mitzvah your Maltese? How can you get in touch with POWARS, the Pet Owners with AIDS/ARC Resource

Service, Inc.? What good "doggie" book should you take with you this weekend for a fun read?

So here we go, every quintessentially New York thing you should know about.

For City Dog Owners with AIDS/ARC

As New Yorkers involved in the lives of people with AIDS know, it is difficult enough to cope with the disease without having to worry about whether or not you will be able to continue to care for your pet. **POWARS, Inc.,** P.O. Box 1116, Madison Square Station, New York, NY 10159, 212-744-0842, is the first and only total-care service for the pets of people with AIDS/ARC in New York City. By supplying assistance at no charge with dog walking, transportation, in-home foster care when owners are in the hospital, and vet care, food, supplies, and grooming on a gratis or sliding-fee scale, POWARS helps people with AIDS keep their pets.

As we all know, the human/animal bond itself is a form of therapy unmatched by treatments or drugs, and too many owners with AIDS have already been separated from their dogs because of misinformation, financial difficulties, fear of illness, and simply the inability to manage several flights of stairs several times a day. With proper planning, and a well-orchestrated corps of volunteers, POWARS's services eliminate the client's anxiety about their animal's well-being, and ensure continuity in the animal's life. POWARS is completely volunteer-dependent, so please do whatever you can to give them a hand. There is no minimum number of hours that you must commit to, and they can always find a way to use someone willing to help out. Naturally, tax-deductible donations are also appreciated and needed.

Therapists

I listed several therapists in chapter eleven who deal specifically with issues dog owners have surrounding the deaths of their pets, but what about therapists who use dogs in their general

Johnathan McCann (left) and Peter Thyne (right) are POWARS volunteers. Th[ey] have shared the work of caring for Chloe the Maltese (center) during her owne[r's] long fight with AIDS. When Chloe's mistress was hospitalized, Chloe would jo[in] either family, playing with Johnathan's Westie, Jeordie, and cavalier King Char[les] spaniel, Sophie, or Peter's two cavaliers, Beatrice and Charlotte. Through the[ir] hard work, Johnathan and Peter made it possible for Chloe's owner to keep a[nd] enjoy her pet despite her battle with AIDS. Credit: Petograp[h]

practice? Freud himself saw patients with his chow chows at his feet and once remarked that his dog Jo-Fi understood what a particular patient needed better than he did. There are New York City therapists who appreciate the human/canine bond and have dogs or other animals at their offices.

Psychoanalyst and psychotherapist **Dr. Joel Gavriele-Gold,** 205 West 89th Street, Office 1A, New York, NY 10024, 212-362-2167, has used his dogs as "co-therapists" for over twenty years. Dr. Gavriele-Gold began including dogs in his practice by chance, when he rescued an abandoned, half-starved poodle-mix puppy from a Manhattan street and was afraid to leave it at home alone. He brought Humphrey to the office, and soon found that his patients got wonderful benefits from having the puppy around.

Humphrey's presence allowed the patients to relate to a non-threatening, compassionate creature, and to express feelings they might withhold from another human being. Humphrey simply lay in the office during sessions, not interfering in the therapy in any way, but Dr. Gavriele-Gold found his quiet contribution remarkable. Humphrey, and Dr. Gavriele-Gold's subsequent dogs, Fergus and Elodie, have an unerring ability to read and react to patients' emotions, as well as the instinct to comfort those in pain—offering a paw on the arm or a head on the lap when necessary. He sees individuals, couples, or groups. Children and adolescents take particular pleasure in the presence of the dogs.

Dog-Friendly Interior Decorators

Dorset Design, Inc., 173 East 80th Street, New York, NY 10021, 212-737-3721, is *the* firm to call if you have pets and are redecorating, reorganizing, or just thinking about getting a new rug. Lovejoy Duryea, and her husband, Bob, have bred dogs for years, initially Labs, now terriers, and Bob is also a governor of the Westminster Kennel Club. They have great experience with many different breeds and *know* how to design, furnish, or reorganize your home for your dog's and your own sanity!

The Duryeas put the pet first, considering the animal's needs as well as your own. If you want carpeting, they'll counsel you about which dyeing process puts the color into the carpet *before* it is woven, so that the rug won't end up with bleached-out areas where your puppy puddled. They have almost magical ways of disguising dog crates, keeping your apartment from looking like a kennel, and arranging your treasures safely away from the potential carnage a wagging tail creates.

As interior designers, they follow the industry and have access to new products benefiting dog owners. For example, they know about a special antimicrobial treatment for fabrics, designed for use in nursing homes, that makes material impermeable to water (no more worries about the "accidents" on the Louis XIV couch). It also keeps dander to a minimum. If you have cats as well, they consider the weave of the fabrics for your furniture and drapes, avoiding those on which cats love to make mischief!

If you have animals in your life and want some guidance in arranging your living space to your pet's and your own best advantage, call them!

Show Biz for Your Dog!

So, your dog is looking up at you with his most adorable expression, and you can't help but think, "He's as beautiful as any of those dogs pictured on the kibble boxes, why isn't my dog a star?"

Well, maybe your dog can "work" in "the business," but listen to my lecture first. You should *only* pursue putting your dog in show biz if your dog genuinely *loves* to work, *loves* people, and if you have the *time* and *energy* to closely supervise the undertaking.

In New York City, there is work for dogs in advertising, television, and as extras in movies. The fees for a dog's services usually range from $100 to $250 a day. If a photographer or art director is looking for, say, a golden retriever to pose with a model and a baby, he or she contacts an animal theatrical agent, who in turn sends over photos of the goldens they represent. The client will select one and "book" the dog through the agent. The dog owner will have to bring the dog to the location of the shoot and supervise the dog's behavior and treatment.

Your dog must be naturally outgoing, thoroughly obedience-trained, and socialized so that he will work under stress and distractions. Competing in dog shows and earning an obedience title is a good way to see if your dog is a "happy worker" and can keep his focus on you regardless of the situation.

Do you have a flexible enough schedule so that you can take a day off if your dog gets a booking? Don't think the agent or your neighbor can just as easily take your dog to the job. You must be available.

Some agents *will* offer to take your dog for the day and simply pay you the $100. Before you jump at the dough, take a moment to think about your dog's welfare. There are no guidelines or rules governing animals working in print or TV. A director can and *will* ask your dog to work, and I don't mean *sit* around the studio, but to *hold* a sit or down stay, maybe under hot lights, or run repeatedly across a backdrop for two hours straight if they want the dog to. The agent values his client—the director—and wants to keep him happy. *You* are the only person sensitive to your dog's interests. Don't allow him to be put in a situation where he may be overworked, or worse, treated abusively by a handler when you aren't there.

If you still think your dog is a good candidate for a career in show biz, then, by all means, call an agent and see what he/she thinks! Remember, *no one* can guarantee that your dog will work, so if any agent asks you for money up front—either for a registration fee or for photographs—your consumer rip-off alarm should sound. It's normal for an agent to ask to see photos of your dog, but good snapshots should be enough to get you started. Same thing for "animal talent workshops," where a trainer will promise to teach your dog tricks that will get her on TV. Again, no one can guarantee that your dog will get work. No doubt he will enjoy the training and extra attention, and if you want to have some fun with your dog learning tricks, these seminars are great. Who knows, something might come of it, but just don't spend your life savings paying for the classes, or blame your dog if he doesn't end up replacing Eddie, the Jack Russell terrier on "Frasier."

Remember that putting your dog with an agent is a business, and very hard work. But if you believe that the two of you are suited for it, here are two agents to contact to get you started:

William Berloni Theatrical Animals Inc.
18 Old Country Road
Higganum, CT 06441
203-345-8734

Dawn Animal Agency
750 Eighth Avenue, Suite 505
New York, NY 10036
212-575-9396

What About Letterman's Stupid Pet Tricks?

If your dog has a talent as unique as the famous vacuum-killing Boston terrier, or the racing dachshunds, he belongs on "The Late Show with David Letterman" in the Stupid Pet Tricks segment. Getting on the show *is* possible! You *do not* need an agent to "introduce" your dog to the casting director, so if a trainer or agent tries to sell you some kind of package on the premise that only they can get your dog on "Letterman," watch out.

If your dog has a remarkable trick, or even a personal mannerism quirky enough to suit Dave's sense of whimsy, give it a shot. Be sure that the dog will do the "trick" on command, under all circumstances, no matter what distractions are present. Then make a videotape of your dog doing whatever it is that he does, and send it with a cover letter introducing yourself, your dog, and describing the trick to:

Susan Hall-Sheehan
Pet & Human Tricks Coordinator
"The Late Show with David Letterman"
1697 Broadway
New York, NY 10019

Fairy tales could come true ... You could find yourself up on the stage with Dave and Paul. Excellent.

Let Your Dog Shed You a New Sweater!

For those of us with dogs who shed prodigiously, Kendall Crolius and Anne Montgomery have come up with a solution. Their book, *Knitting with Dog Hair* (St. Martin's Press, 1994), urges you to "Stop vacuuming, start knitting!" Apparently it all started when Kendall Crolius couldn't get sheep's wool in Brooklyn and decided to give the silken fluff her golden retriever was "donating" a try. Sure enough, after carding, twisting, and weaving, the dog's hair came out very much like cashmere. Who knew? Obviously some breeds' hair lends itself to the process better than others',—Samoyed hair is divine to knit with, but if you've got a weimeraner, forget about it! The book will give you complete instructions, so have fun.

If you collect the rich undercoat your dog sheds, **Creature Comforts,** P.O. Box 606, Vashon, WA 98070, will do the work of carding and hand-spinning the fluff. They will also knit or weave garments and blankets from your dog's yarn to your specifications. Send them a stamped, self-addressed envelope to receive more information.

Great Doggie Reads and Where to Get Them

There is marvelous literature about our canine friends. The master, of course, is James Thurber, whose dog stories have been collected in *Thurber's Dogs* (Fireside, Simon & Schuster, 1992), a not-to-be-missed, soon-to-be-dog-eared (when you're forced to put it down) book.

I've mentioned the works of Vicki Hearne, but *Animal Happiness* (HarperCollins, 1994), her most recent book, and her very first book, *Adam's Task: Calling Animals By Name* (HarperPerennial), should be on every dog lover's bookshelf.

A Dog Is Listening: The Way Some of Our Closest Friends View Us, by Roger Caras (Summit Books, 1992), is a charming, thoughtful compendium of stories, history, and musings about the nature of the canine/human bond. A lovely book to keep on your bedside table for late-night reading.

If you love dogs, and you love suspense, the Dog Lover's Mystery Series by Susan Conant is for you! Heroine Holly Winter and her Alaskan malamutes find intrigue at every turn. What makes these books so special are the little details and descriptions of and about our canine pals. Try one of them out for a weekend read, and you might get hooked! Books in the series include *Dead and Doggone, A New Leash on Death, A Bite of Death, Paws Before Dying, Gone to the Dogs,* and *Bloodlines* (published by Doubleday).

The Quotable Canine, by Paul Coughlin and Jim Dratfield (Doubleday, 1995), is the coffee-table dog book to die for. Famous quotes about our beloved canines are accompanied by gorgeous photos of dogs, done by Coughlin and Dratfield, of Petography Inc. (See page 189 on where to have portraits of your dog taken to hire Petography to photograph your dog!)

Blue Dog, by George Rodrigue and Lawrence Freundlich (Viking Studio Books, 1994), contains the beautiful, mystical paintings by George Rodrigue and a wonderful story about how his dog continued to visit him in dreams, leading him on a marvelous journey. Not to be missed.

Where to Get Those Books

The Dog Lover's Bookshop, 9 West 31st Street, 2nd floor, New York, NY 10018, 212-594-3601, is open from 12:00 to 6:00 P.M., Monday through Saturday, and sells new and out-of-print books, video and audiotapes, cards, calendars, and gifts—about dogs. Their children's department even has canine coloring books and rubber stamps. It's a delightful shop where your dog is most welcome!

Bibliography of the Dog, P.O. Box 118, Churubusco, NY 12932, 514-827-2717, fax: 514-827-2091, offers a large selection of rare and out-of-print books about dogs. They have fiction and illustrated works, poetry, general reference, books on dogs in sports and fashion, Seeing Eye dogs, dogs at war, and more.

The **American Kennel Club,** 51 Madison Avenue, 20th floor, New York, NY 10010, 212-696-8246, has a marvelous library, not only full of over 16,000 wonderful books and texts concerning dogs and their history, but an informal art gallery that fills the halls. Works by the "masters" of canine portraiture are displayed, including Maud Earl, Sir Edwin Landseer, and Gustav Muss-Arnoldt.

Where to Find Doggie Furnishings, Art, and Antiques

For "things doggie" for the home, you must start at **Mabel's,** 849 Madison Avenue, New York, NY 10021, between 70th and 71st streets, 212-734-3263. They have the *most wonderful* collection of canine (and feline) furniture, chests, picture frames, sculpture, paintings, and just general *stuff*! Most of the items are hand-painted and all are extraordinarily wonderful. Just look for the famous awning on Madison Avenue with the giant black and white cat's face on it, and you'll have found Mabel's.

Although I mentioned this shop in chapter three, remember that **Karen's for People & Pets,** 1195 Lexington Avenue, New York, NY 10028, 212-472-9440, has hand-painted furniture by Bill Easton. The store has a great selection of mirrors, toy boxes, and beds for dogs, all of which can be customized or personalized.

By special order, **Carlyle Custom Convertibles, Inc.,** 1056 Third Avenue, New York, NY 10021, 212-838-1525, makes the "Puppy Palace," the *last word* in posh dog accommodations. Inspired by an antique dog bed on display in the Wrightsman Room at the Metropolitan Museum of Art, the "Puppy Palace" is a 16-by-20-inch dog bed ensconced in an enclosed canopy frame suitable for a rajah! It can be done in any fabric and trim. Clearly, the "Puppy Palace" is only for smaller breeds, but it gives your dog a niche to snuggle in, fitting elegantly in the most sumptuously decorated room. I understand that the "Puppy Palace" is the New York celebrity's and socialite's gift of choice for their beloved lapdogs.

In the Company of Dogs, 800-964-3647, is a terrific new catalogue that presents dog products in a lifestyle setting. You'll find stylish dog beds, a pet ottoman in home decor fabrics, dog motif accent pillows, home accessories, jewelry, and holiday gifts—that can often be personalized—for both dogs and their owners.

William Secord Gallery, 52 East 76th Street, between Park and Madison avenues, New York, NY 10021, 212-249-0075, specializes in dog art. They show paintings and sculpture in which canines are center stage. It is also possible to commission one of their marvelous artists to paint your dog in the classic style of eighteenth- and nineteenth-century dog portraiture. The gallery represents artists who do exquisite portraiture in the classic formal style of the eighteenth and nineteenth centuries. These oil and watercolor paintings are expensive, but will become instant treasures. A visit to this extraordinary gallery is a treat for any dog fancier!

Frank J. Miele Gallery, 1262 Madison Avenue, New York, NY 10028, 212-876-5775, represents fifty American artists who use dogs as themes and subjects for their paintings and sculptures.

All Creatures Great and Small, Ltd., P.O. Box 355, Congers, NY 10920, 800-862-9684, offers the very best china and porcelain dog and animal figures by Royal Doulton, Worchester, Hutchenreuther, Crown Derby, Crown Dalton, and Copenhagen. The pieces are very beautiful and make marvelous presents for other dog people.

Priscilla Snyder, 3 Hanover Square, New York, NY 10004, 212-344-2209, is a gifted artist who has developed a technique of working so vividly with embroidery that it's like painting with thread. Snyder uses her art on beautiful, realistic-looking handbags, briefcases, and suitcases. By literally painting a portrait of your pet in thread, the bag looks as though you have your dog at your side! The works are expensive, but should be considered as art—a one-of-a-kind soft sculpture—rather than as an accessory.

Alice Kwartler Antiques, 123 East 57th Street, New York, NY 10022, between Park and Lexington avenues, 212-752-3590. When you're window-shopping along 57th Street, *do not* miss this gem of an antiques shop. Alice has a soft spot for our canine friends and is always on the lookout for "things doggie." The pieces change constantly, but recently she had nineteenth-century sterling and enamel decorative boxes with dog portraits on the top, sterling compacts, and dog motif money clips.

Bonnie Lewis, Jewelry of Animal Design, 8956 County Road 250, Durango, CO 81301, 303-247-1549. This gorgeous collection of antique doggie jewelry features items like a pair of circa 1910 fourteen-carat gold and English crystal cufflinks with a dachshund's face in the crystal, a circa 1880 twenty-two-carat gold and English crystal dog pin/pendant and stickpin featuring a King Charles spaniel, or an *amazing* circa 1940 charm bracelet in ten-, fourteen-, and eighteen-carat gold with AKC champion ribbons and tiny dog statues of different breeds. The collection is a feast for the eyes. Send for a catalogue.

The Dog Museum, 1721 South Mason Road, St. Louis, MO 63131, 314-821-3647, is "dedicated to the exhibition and interpretation of the art, artifacts, and literature of the dog."

They publish a beautiful museum gift catalogue that features dog-oriented art, literature, jewelry, and collectibles. From "Dogs of the World Playing Cards" (a different breed on each card) and dog suspenders to an Oscar de la Renta silk scarf featuring various breeds, and a line of wonderful wearable art pins of dog angels (these are also available as hanging tree decorations in their Christmas catalogue). The whole collection is gorgeous and not to be missed.

DOG GOODS LTD., 2035 West Wabansia, Chicago, IL 60647, 800-736-4746, is mentioned in the chapter on supplies for their many classic and functional canine items, but they also have a few extraordinary things for owners too. The handy canvas carry-all bags with dog and animal motifs will serve you from town to country. They also carry the work of well-known equine artist Nancy Baldwin, who will do customized portraiture on trunks, chairs, boxes, and frames.

Where to Have Portraiture of Your Dog Done

Petography Inc., 25 Central Park West, New York, NY 10023, 212-245-0914. I was lucky enough to have the incredible talents of Petography photographer Paul Coughlin and art director Jim Dratfield involved with the photos in this book. Paul and Jim usually work in their signature fine-art sepia prints. They use archival and acid-free materials, assuring that the precious photos of your pet will last. As gifted with animals as they are as artists, Paul and Jim always capture the essence of their canine subject.

Theresa Cannon-King at **Fur Faces,** 212-929-2430, also does charming photos of New York pets.

A unique and classic medium for a portrait of your dog is polished black granite. **Stone Imagery,** P.O. Box 2645, Carlsbad, CA 92018, 619-434-4493, does *the most* beautiful "photoengravature" on polished black granite. The effect is stunning, and the finished piece can be displayed on a small decorative easel or set in concrete in a garden or in your fireplace. You can have a caption or personal message of any sort added as well. The cost is around $150. Call for their brochure—you will be impressed.

The Pet Department Store, 233 West 54th Street, New

York, NY 10019, 212-489-9195, also represents artists and can find you one who suits your dog and your pocketbook!

Illustrator and artist **Glenna Hartwell,** 119 Philhaven Avenue, Califon, NJ 07830, 908-832-6684, does gorgeous oil paintings of dogs, and her work has appeared in numerous books and magazines. She works carefully with you and your dog doing sittings and taking photographs so that the finished piece of artwork truly reflects your pet's character.

Dogs Online

For computer owners, an entire world of dog information is available online. Thousands of owners, trainers, breeders, and fanciers log on each day, meeting electronically to exchange advice and debate issues relating to dogs. Some of the canine online services you can subscribe to are **America Online:** The Pet Forum, 800-827-6364; **CompuServe:** Pets/Animals Forum, Time Warner Dog and Cat Forum, and The Humane Society Forum, 800-848-8199; **DOGNET:** dog-only service, 800-DOGNET; **Prodigy:** Pets Bulletin Board, 800-776-3449.

If you receive e-mail there are several wonderful discussion groups of a doggie nature. Canine-L is a great one. You can join by writing an e-mail with "subscribe Canine-L" in the subject line to listserv@psuvm.binet.

You can receive a complete listing of all dog-related e-mail lists—from Agility-L, for those who enjoy competing in agility work with their dogs, to Shy-K9s, for owners coping with the particular problems of shy or nervous dogs. This master list of lists can be found by sending a request to "mail-server@rtfm.mit.edu", with "send usenet/news.answers/dogs-faq/email-list" in the body of the e-mail message. Have fun—you will join a wonderful community of dog people—but you will have a *full* mailbox.

Dog Radio

Although television shows about dogs pop up every so often, there is nothing quite as certain, or as useful, as **"The Pet Show,"** Saturday afternoons on WOR Radio (AM 710); call

212-642-4500 for program information. Hosted by wonderful pet expert/author/personality Dr. Warren Eckstein, *The Pet Show* mixes animal-related information and news with plenty of call-in questions from listeners. Dr. Eckstein is as entertaining as he is informative, and it's fun to hear other New Yorkers talk to him about their pets.

Just Neat Stuff You Should Know About

Picture *New York* magazine, but for your dog. If you're not reading *PETHOUSE* magazine by now, you should be. This bimonthly is full of the latest information for New York City canines, from articles on animal care and new products to listings of events. Call **212-679-1850** to find out the nearest city location where you can pick up a copy.

How can I describe **Lee Day**, 201-748-6420, the celebrity pet groomer and pet entertainer? A "true" combination of Broadway belle and dog lover, her mottoes are: "Let me sing your dog clean!" and "Your dog is MY celebrity." Lee does grooming all over the tri-state area, specializing in tender treatment for elderly or disabled pets. What makes Lee a New York original are the "events" she'll throw for your pet.

She will design, produce, and perform at any occasion you can dream up. She has bark mitzvahed Joan Rivers's beloved dog, Spike, on TV, and has performed all manner of doggie weddings, birthday parties, dates, honeymoons, baptisms, and baby showers! Lee is very creative and has a wonderful seamstress who makes the clothes for the animals! Whatever the occasion, Lee will find an entertaining, delightfully wacky way to celebrate it. Call her. She's a peach.

Blue Ribbons Pet Products, 75 Modular Avenue, Commack, NY 11725, 516-785-0640, puts out a great catalogue of doggie things, but of particular interest are its "Forever Paws" pet paw print kits. As adorable as your child's handprint, paw print kits come complete with nontoxic, pliable bronze "paw dough" that takes incredibly detailed impressions of your pet's paw. A personalized heart-shaped plaque is included to display the paw print!

Poochie Presents Dog Treat of the Month Club, 1559 North LaSalle, Suite 241, Chicago, IL 60610, 800-FUN-DOGS, is just what it sounds like, a monthly delivery of scrumptious morsels to your favorite canine. The treats are all-natural and they include special items for your pet's birthday and holidays!

The Paw Pals Club, P.O. Box 5641, Station A, Wilmington, NC 28403, is the original International Pet Correspondence Club, or pet pen pals! Why not have a correspondence with a dog lover in another country? Send the club a postcard, and they'll send you an information kit.

Dogs in Church?

Holy Trinity Episcopal Church, on East 88th Street, between 1st and 2nd avenues, 212-289-4100, encourages dog owners to bring their pets to the 8:15 A.M. Sunday morning service. No more excuses that you have to walk the dog! Now you can take your dog out *and* go to church regularly. It's a wonderfully loving and inclusive idea that honors the special roles our pets play in our lives.

The Blessing of the Animals

Many churches offer a blessing of the animals service every year on October 4, St. Francis of Assisi day. St. Francis is the patron saint of animals (for the ultimate St. Francis, go see the painting *St. Francis in the Desert* by Giovanni Bellini in the Frick Collection, 1 East 70th Street, New York, NY 10021). Although most churches don't hold special services, a clergy member will usually accommodate you. I was told that if I brought my dog to St. Patrick's Cathedral on that day and asked for the priest on duty, he would oblige us with a special prayer and blessing.

The Cathedral of St. John the Divine, Amsterdam Avenue at 111th Street, has the grandest event, an Earth Mass followed by the blessing—a parade/pageant in which camels and horses join dogs, cats, budgies, and teddy bears in a march to the altar to be blessed. Not to be missed, even if you don't have an animal!

Christmas Eve Blessing of the Animals, Central Presbyterian Church, 593 Park Avenue at 64th Street; 7:00 P.M. wor-ship service. This is the *most* sublime way to pass Christmas Eve! Join this magical congregation full of dogs and other pets, assembled each year to recognize the creatures in our lives, and the presence of animals in the Christmas story. The service concludes with each animal receiving a blessing at the altar.

Yearly Calendar of New York Dog Miscellany and Events

JANUARY

All month: Save tender paws from salty, icy pavements with Musher's Wax, an easily applied, non-staining wax, which seals and protects your pet's feet from a case of "New York sore paw." Available at better supply stores.

FEBRUARY

Second week: WESTMINSTER! Madison Square Garden

The biggie! Considered the most prestigious dog show in the nation. A veritable canine feast as the best dogs of the various breeds compete for honors. There is also a doggie fair of sorts that accompanies the show, at which manufacturers of canine supplies and services offer their wares. Just go!

Valentine's Day: Heart-shaped dog treats from Bakery Soutine, 104 West 70th Street, New York, NY 10023, 212-496-1450

For your special canine valentine, the Rosenbergs, who run this exceptional French bakery, ably assisted by their black Lab, Huckleberry, offer delicious heart-shaped dog treats with your dog's name in icing. These treats are also the perfect present for your puppy to give *his* special canine valentines! Get yourself something scrumptious while you're there—BUT REMEMBER, NO CHOCOLATE FOR YOUR POOCH!

MARCH

18th: Serena's birthday!

Be sure to celebrate your dog's birthday with a party, toys, and a cake—see the recipe below! You can also have someone else do all the work—The Pet Department Store, 233 W. 54th Street, 212-489-9195, and Pampered Paws, 227 E. 57th Street, 212-935-7297, regularly throw "doggie bashes" celebrating canine birthdays or other events!

APRIL

All month: Meet the Easter bunny at Karen's for People & Pets, 1195 Lexington Avenue, New York, NY 10028, 212-472-9440.

Karen persuades the Easter bunny to make an appearance at her shop every Easter season. Your dog can even pose for a souvenir photo with the huge hare!

Doggie Party Cake

This is a basic meatloaf-type recipe which can be used as a dog birthday or holiday cake depending on how you decorate it.

3 pounds ground turkey
2 eggs (or 3 egg whites)
1½ cups oatmeal
Dash of garlic powder
¼ cup minced parsley

Mix ingredients thoroughly. Mold into desired shape (a ring is especially easy for several dogs to eat). Bake at 350 degrees in a pan or on a rack on a cookie sheet, for between 45 minutes to 1 hour 15 minutes, depending on thickness of cake. Remove from oven and cool. Frost with low-fat cream cheese tinted with food coloring if desired. Decorate with cream cheese squeezed through a pastry tube and dog treats.

**Third weekend: The New York Pet Expo, Rock-
land Community College, Suffern, NY 10901;
call 800-955-7469 for information.**

For pet lovers of all ages, this show has exhibits of
pet products, pet services, breeders, a petting zoo for
the kids, pony rides, and animal awareness groups.

MAY

**First Sunday: Paws Walk Against Cancer, River-
side Park, at the Soldiers' and Sailors' Monument, 84th Street and Riverside Drive.**

A noncompetitive walkathon to benefit the American
Cancer Society and the Donaldson-Atwood Cancer Center
Clinic at the Animal Medical Center. A wonderful day!
Booths, entertainment, prizes, and refreshment, as well as
a "talent search" by CBS's "Late Show with David Letterman" for Stupid Pet Tricks. It's great fun and an opportunity to raise critically needed funds while celebrating the
unique bond between humans and animals.

**Second Wednesday: Channel 5's "Good Day New
York Annual Mutt Show"; 6:30 A.M. at the northeast corner of the Great Lawn in Central Park.**

A hilarious chance to get your "mutt"—no purebreds,
please—and your mug on TV! The three categories your
dog may enter are: Best Frisbee Catcher (pretty obvious);
Mutt That Looks Most Like Its Owner (yes, dressing alike
does help in this category); and Most Disobedient Mutt
(which last year meant funny man Soupy Sales yelling
commands at the confused entrants, which none of them
obeyed, and complaining that even dogs didn't listen to
him!). The whole thing is broadcast live on Channel 5's
"Good Day New York," and it's a lot of fun!

**Second Sunday: K9 DAY, Hudson River Park,
Gansevoort and West streets, Manhattan.**

To benefit The Humane Society of the United
States, and organized by the Big Apple Triathalon Club
and the Hudson River Park Conservancy, this
run/walkathon offers dog lovers a chance to take part in
either a one-mile fun run or a two-mile walk. Other
activities include demonstrations of obedience, agility,

guide dog training, and pet therapy, as well as a pet product expo. Lots of fun for all!

Third Saturday: "You Gotta Have Park" Pets, People & Parks Walkathon, Van Cortlandt Parade Ground, W. 246th Street and Broadway, the Bronx.

To benefit the Friends of Van Cortlandt Park and the Delta Society, this noncompetitive walkathon is chaired by master dog trainer Bash Dibra, who has his very successful business, Fieldston Pets, in the community. The day is full of fun and events, an owner/dog look-alike contest, smart pet tricks, and more! Take your pet to enjoy and support beautiful Van Cortlandt Park and raise funds for the Delta Society.

JUNE

First Saturday: Paws Across the Hamptons Dog Walk, Ball Field, Bridgehampton, NY; to benefit ARF and Bide-A-Wee

These two wonderful organizations, ARF, the Animal Rescue Fund of the Hamptons, and the Bide-A-Wee Home Association, which has two shelters on the island, do wonderful things for homeless and abandoned dogs and cats. This fund-raising walkathon is the kickoff for a summer of fun events. Come, enjoy the day, and help two very worthy causes!

JULY

July 4: Please be sensitive to your dog's fear of firecrackers and fireworks. The unexpected explosions can traumatize your pet. Don't force him outside in the noise, and keep your windows closed and music on in your apartment to muffle the sounds outside.

Last Two Saturdays: ARF Celebrity Tennis Tournament, Hampton Athletic Club and The Racquet Club of East Hampton Summer Celebrity Tournament benefiting the Animal Rescue Fund of the Hamptons.

AUGUST

All month long: If you're stuck in town, remember how hot New York pavement can be on paws! Give your dog plenty of water, and keep the A/C or a fan on all day.

SEPTEMBER

Third Wednesday: The Dog Party, The Corner Bookstore, 1313 Madison Avenue at 93rd Street, 6:00 to 8:00 P.M.

A not-to-be-missed gathering of dogs and their owners, The Corner Bookstore throws this wonderful shindig for New York dogs.

OCTOBER

Designated "Adopt a Dog Month" by The American Humane Society!

First Sunday: St. Francis of Assisi Day, blessing of the animals, Cathedral of St. John the Divine, West 111th Street and Amsterdam Avenue.

Let your dog join the festival parade of elephants, camels, horses, and many other animals as they progress through the largest Gothic cathedral in the western hemisphere to be blessed at the altar. A joyous combination of circus and religious ritual.

Second Saturday: Dachshund Octoberfest! Washington Square Park, sponsored by the Dachshund Friendship Club, 212-475-5512.

Come to Washington Square Park and see the most amazing congregation of canine vertebrae in New York City. They're long, low, and lovely, and they even parade around the park in the Grand March of the Dachshunds. Not to be missed!

Third Sunday: Woofstock! The ASPCA Walkathon, Rumsey Band Shell, Central Park.

The original noncompetitive walkathon/fund-raiser to benefit the ASPCA. A great day of fun and activities for walkers and supporters of the "A." Celebrity dog-owner appearances, contests and demonstrations, booths of doggie stuff, and more.

Halloween: the Saturday before, psychic readings, The Pet Bar, 98 Thompson Street between Prince and Spring streets, SoHo, 212-274-0510.

Every Halloween this downtown pet shop hires an animal psychic to communicate telepathically with your pets. She'll give you the lowdown on what your dog really thinks, either in person or by using a photo you bring her! So entertaining and popular that you should arrive early to get a place in line!

NOVEMBER

First weekend: Long Island Pet Expo, Nassau Coliseum, Uniondale, LI.

More exhibits, pet services, breeders, et cetera.

Thanksgiving: Macy's Thanksgiving Day Parade, 72nd Street and Central Park West, down Broadway to 34th Street.

You've watched it on TV, but when there's good weather, the Macy's parade is a lot of fun to attend with your dog. Of course there are incredible crowds, but if you can get a spot with your pet inside Central Park on a hill so that you can see everything, it's a blast. Remember to be sensitive to your dog if the loud drums of the marching bands sound too much like thunder for his "comfort level."

DECEMBER

All month: Give the Gift of Love, The Humane Society, 300 East 59th Street, New York, NY 10022.

During the holiday season, this wonderful shelter has a very special drive during which they ask New York animal lovers to donate toys, treats, even blankets and beds for the dogs and cats (and birds!) without homes who must pass the holidays in the shelter. While you're out shopping for your pet, why not pick up something extra for a Humane Society pal!

All month: Meet Santa Claus at Karen's for People & Pets, 1195 Lexington Avenue, New York, NY 10028, 212-472-9440.

Yes, Kris Kringle gives your pet the chance to sit on or by Santa's knee and tell him what dog toys and treats should appear in his doggie stocking. Of course a photographer is present to capture the moment!

Christmas Week: Prospect Park Dog Walkers Carol Sing, Park Slope, Brooklyn.

Join other dogs and their owners in a jolly carol sing. It may be cold, but spirits will rise as you walk and sing while your dogs socialize!

Christmas Eve Blessing of the Animals: Central Presbyterian Church, 593 Park Avenue at 64th Street; 7:00 P.M.

Join this magical congregation and pass a sublime Christmas Eve with your dog at your side.

New Year's Eve: After Halloween, this has become the second most popular "dress up your pet" night of the year. Most of the shops and grooming salons selling doggie duds offer tuxedos and gowns for your pet. Why not let him ring in the New Year in style?

With these suggestions, I hope to see you taking your dog out on the town! There's no place like New York for dogs and their owners. We have access to the most creative and pleasurable events—the opportunity to live it up in the company of our dogs! So plan that doggie birthday party! Visit the AKC library! Lend a hand to the wonderful people at POWARS! Get out to one or more of the many walkathons for doggie causes! Just take your dog by the paw and have some fun!

A Christmas Eve gathering, where all faiths are welcome, at Manhattan's Central Presbyterian Church for a blessing of the animals. Reverend Richard Pindar holds Lucy in his lap, surrounded by parishioners Marion Finger (left) with her dog, Schatzi, Lee Tanny (right) holding Lovey, the dachshund, Giorgio, the collie, and Serena. Every Christmas Eve at 7 P.M. a magical congregation of animals and their owners enjoy a special service honoring the creatures of the earth and their role in the Christmas story. The service ends with the animals coming to the altar to be blessed and then going out into the cold New York night full of the warmth and sharing of Christmas.

Credit: Petography